The Book of Courage

by

John Thomson Faris

FOREWORD

A TEACHER has told of the greatest moment of discouragement that ever came to her. At cost of great labor she had fitted up a room for the use of children, placing pictures on the walls, plants in the windows, goldfish on the table, and a canary in a cage. But the night before the day when she planned to welcome the children to the room there was a cold snap, and the janitor let the fire go out. In the morning she looked on broken radiators, frozen goldfish, drooping plants, and what she feared was a dead bird. In her despair she was about to decide that she would never make another effort to have things pleasant for the children, when the bit of fluff in the bird-cage, roused from stupor by the noise made by the discouraged woman, lifted its voice in song.

That song told her that she had reached once again the point that comes to everyone, times without number, the point that separates the life of conquest from the life of defeat, the life of cowardice from the life of courage. She was at the crossroads, and she took the turning to the right. The bird's song marked for her the end of discouragement.

"I can sing, as well as the bird," she said to herself. And at once she began to make plans for her charges.

Everywhere there are people who feel that the odds are against them, that difficulties in the way are unsurmountable, that it is useless to make further effort to conquer. The author of "The Book of Courage" knows by experience how they feel, and he longs to send to them a message of cheer and death-to-the-blues, a call to go on to the better things that wait for those who face life in the spirit of the gallant General Petain, whose watchword, "They shall not pass!" put courage into his men and hope into the hearts of millions all over the world.

"Courage!" is the call to these. "Courage" is likewise the word to those who are already struggling in the conquering spirit of Sir Walter Scott who, when both domestic calamity and financial misfortune came, said to a comforter, "The blowing off of my hat on a stormy day has given me more weariness," who called adversity "a tonic and a bracer."

The world needs courage—the high courage that shows itself in a life of daily struggle and conquest, that smiles at obstacles and laughs at difficulties.

How is the needed courage to be secured? What are the springs of courage? What are some of the results of courage? These are questions "The Book of Courage" seeks to answer by telling of men and women who have become courageous.

Glorious provision has been made by the Inspirer of men for giving courage to all, no matter what their difficulties or their hardships. Among His provisions are home and friends, work and service, will and conscience, the world with all its beauty, and Himself as Companion and Friend.

Thus we are left absolutely without excuse when we are tempted to let down the bars to worry and gloom and discouragement.

Keep up the bars! Don't let the enemies of peace and progress pass! And always,

> "Like the star,
> That shines afar,
> Without haste,
>   And without rest,
> Let each man wheel, with steady sway
> Round the tasks that rule the day,
>   And do his best."

J. T. F.

PHILADELPHIA, 1920

CHAPTER ONE

THE COURAGE OF SELF-CONQUEST

THE highest courage is impossible without self-conquest. And self-conquest is never easy. A man may be a marvel of physical courage, and be a coward in matters of self-government. Failure here threatens dire disaster to his entire career.

Alexander the Great conquered most of the world he knew, but he permitted his lower nature to conquer his better self, and he died a disappointed, defeated man.

Before the days of Alexander there was a man named Nehemiah from whom the world-conqueror might have learned a few secrets. He was a poor exile in the service of a foreign ruler. That ruler sent him down to Jerusalem, the capital city of his own home land, with instructions to govern the people there. Now, in those days, it was a common thing for governors of cities to plunder the people unfortunate enough to be in their charge. Thus Nehemiah would have had ample precedent to fill his own coffers by injustice, profiteering and worse: he had the power. Possibly he was tempted to do something of the sort. But he had the courage to shut up tight all baser passions, and then to sit firmly on the lid. In the brief record of his service he referred to some of the self-seeking governors, and told of their rascally deeds. Then he added the significant words, "*So did not I.* "

That was certainly courage—the courage of self-conquest.

As a young man Ulysses S. Grant was a brave soldier, but he nearly wrecked his life because of weak yielding to his appetite. His real career began only with self-conquest. When he found the courage to fight himself —and not until then—he became ready for the marvelous life of high courage that never faltered when he was misunderstood by associates and maligned by enemies, that pressed steadily onward, in the face of biting disease, until work was done, until honor was satisfied.

I
RESTRAINING SELF

A little girl four years old came trembling to her mother and asked for pencil and paper. Then, teeth set and eyes flashing, she pounced on the paper and began to make all sorts of vicious marks. Asked what she was doing, she said she was writing a letter to a sister who had offended her by an act that had been misunderstood. "She is not a nice girl," the little critic said, "and I'm telling her so. I don't like her any more, and I'm saying that." As she wrote her hand trembled; she was carried away by her unpleasant emotion. After a few moments, unable to go on with her self-appointed task, she flung herself, sobbing, into her mother's arms and for half an hour she could not control herself.

The sight was pitiful. But far more pitiful is the spectacle of one old enough to know better who yields to vexation and hatred, thereby not only making himself disagreeable, but robbing himself of power to perform the duties of the hour. For there is nothing so exhausting as uncontrolled emotion. There is so much for each one of us to do, and every ounce of strength is needed by those who would play their part in the world. Then what spendthrift folly it is to waste needed power on emotion that is disquieting, disagreeable and disgraceful!

That lesson was never impressed more forcibly than by a French officer of whom a visitor from America asked, "Did I understand that you had lost three sons?" "Yes, sir, and two brothers," was the proud reply. "How you must hate the Boche," remarked a bystander. "No, no," was the instant reply, "not hate; just pity, sir; pity, but not hate. Hate, you know, is an excessive emotion, sir; and no one can do effective work if he spends his vitality in an excess of emotion. No," he concluded, "we cannot hate; we cannot work if we burn up ourselves inside. Pity, sir; pity. 'They know not what they do.' That's the idea. And they don't."

The same lesson of self-restraint was taught by Marshal Foch in his words to the soldiers of France. He urged them to keep their eyes and ears ready and their mouths "in the safety notch"; and he told them they must obey orders first and kick afterwards if they had been wronged. He said,

"Bear in mind that the enemy is your enemy and the enemy of humanity until he is killed or captured; then he is your dear brother or fellow soldier beaten or ashamed, whom you should no further humiliate." He told them that it was necessary to keep their heads clear and cool, to be of good cheer, to suffer in silence, to dread defeat, but not wounds, to fear dishonor, but not death, and to die game. Because so many of the soldiers under him heeded this wise admonition, they did not waste their precious strength on useless and harmful emotions, but they were ever ready to go to their task, with the motto of their division, "It shall be done."

What a blessing it will be to the world that millions of young men were trained in France to repress hurtful emotion, to exercise self-restraint—which may be defined as the act or process of holding back or hindering oneself from harmful thoughts or actions. And what a wonderful thing it will be if the lesson is passed on to us, so that we shall not be like the torrent that wastes its power by rushing and brawling over the stones, all to no purpose, but like the harnessed stream whose energy is made to turn the wheels of factory and mill. For only guarded and guided strength is useful and safe.

II
EFFACING SELF

"Every man that falls must understand beforehand that he is a dead man and nothing can save him. It is useless for him to cry out, and it may, by giving the alarm, cause the enterprise to fail."

This was the message to his men of the officer to whom Napoleon committed the capture of Mt. Cenis.

The historian tells us that at one point in the ascent of a precipitous track, three men fell. "Their bodies were heard bounding from crag to crag, but not a cry was heard, not a moan. The body of one hero was recovered later. There was a smile on his lips."

How that record of the silence succeeded by a smile grips the heart, for it was not the false courage that plays to the grandstand, but the deeper, truer courage that sinks self for the good of others, and does this not merely because it is a part of the game, but with the gladness that transfigures life.

Such courage does not wait for some great occasion for exhibiting itself; it is revealed in the midst of the humdrum routine of daily life—a routine that is especially trying to those who have been looking forward to some great, perhaps dramatic service.

A young man of seventeen entered the navy, with his parents' consent, as an apprentice. When he left home he had dreams of entering at once on a life of thrilling adventure where there would be numberless opportunities for the display of high courage. At the end of a month a friend asked him how he liked life at the navy yard. "Fine!" was the reply. "What are you doing?" was the next query. "They haven't given me anything but window washing to do yet," he replied, with a smile that was an index of character.

A newspaper writer has told of a college student nineteen years old who enlisted in the navy. He was sent to one of our naval stations and told to guard a pile of coal. As the summer passed he still guarded that coal pile. He wrote home about it:

"You know, dad, when we were little shavers, you always rubbed it into us that anything that was worth doing at all was worth doing as well as it could be done. I've been standing over that coal pile nearly three months now, and it looks just exactly as small as it did when I first landed on the job."

"He was relieved from the coal pile at last and promoted," said the writer who told of him. "At the same time the government gave him a last chance to return to his college work. He thought it over carefully. He realized that America was going to need trained men as never before, but still, he decided, the best service that he individually could give was the one that he had chosen. He had a few days of leave before going on to his next assignment, and he hurried back to his home. He found that his summer task was a matter of town history, and he had to face a good deal of affectionate raillery about his coal pile. Of course he did not mind that. But his answer revealed his spirit:

"'You may laugh, but that coal pile was all right. I'll admit it got on my nerves for a bit, but I figured it out that while I was taking care of that coal pile I was releasing some other fellow who knew things I didn't know, and who could do things I couldn't do. I'm ready to stand by a coal pile till the war ends, if that's where I can help the most.'"

"That is the spirit that will conquer because it is the spirit that never can be conquered," was the comment made on the incident. "There is no self in it—only consecration to duty; no seeking for large things—only for an opportunity to serve whenever the call comes. That is the spirit that is growing in America to-day—and only through such spirit can we accomplish our great task in the life of the world."

The man who really desires to serve his fellows does not think of declaring that he will not do humble tasks, but he demands that the work he is asked to do shall be needed.

A young man who was seeking his life work made known his willingness to be a shoe-black, if he could be convinced that this was the work God wanted him to do. An immigrant in New York City read in the morning, "Lord, my heart is not haughty nor mine eyes lofty." Then he went out to sweep a store, and he swept it well. It is worthy of note that the young man who was willing to be a shoe-black became one of the foremost men of his generation, and that the immigrant became the pastor of a leading city church. But a far more important fact is that the quality of the service given counted more in their minds than the character of the employment.

The service of the man who would be worth while in the world must partake of the spirit of the successful figure on the baseball diamond or the football gridiron: readiness to do everything, or anything—or to do nothing, if he is so directed—in the interests of the team. It must take a leaf from the book of General Pershing and his fellow officers who, in a time of stress for the Allies, were willing and eager to brigade their troops with the soldiers of France and England, thus losing the identity of their forces in the interest of the great cause for which they stood. It must learn the lesson taught by the life of Him who emptied Himself for the sake of the world—and did it with a smile.

III
FORGIVING INJURIES

A gifted writer has told the story of a workman in a Bessemer steel furnace who was jealous of the foreman whom he thought had injured him. The foreman was making a good record, and the workman did not want to see him succeed. So he plotted his undoing—he loosened the bolts of the cable that controlled an important part of the machinery, and so caused an accident that not only interfered seriously with the day's turn, but put a section of the plant out of commission for the time being. As a result the superintendent was discharged. When he left he vowed vengeance on the man whom he suspected of causing his discharge: "I'll get you for this some day," he declared. Perhaps he would have been even more emphatic if he had known the extent of his enemy's culpability.

Years passed. The workman who had loosened the bolts became superintendent of the mill. He, too, tried to break a production record, and was in a fair way to succeed until some mysterious difficulty developed that interfered seriously with results. And just when the new superintendent was losing sleep over his problem, the old superintendent came to town.

"He's come for his revenge!" was the thought of the new superintendent.

But the superintendent did not wait for a visit from the man he feared; he sought him at once. "He must know the extent of my meanness," he decided. So he told his story. To his surprise the former foreman seemed more interested in the account of the progress of the mill than in the sorry tale of past misdeeds. Learning of the mysterious difficulty that threatened failure in the attempt to break the production record, the injured man showed real concern. "I can't imagine where the difficulty is, but I'd like to take a look around for it," he said. Arm in arm, then, the two men, once bitter enemies, moved toward the mill. The search was successful, the difficulty was corrected, and the record was broken.

Fine story, isn't it? What a pity it is only a story, that such things don't ever happen in real life!

Don't they? How about Henry Nasmyth, the English inventor of the steam piledriver, whose ideas were stolen by French machinists? His first knowledge of the piracy was when he saw a crude imitation of his piledriver in a factory in France. Instead of seeking damages and threatening vengeance, he pointed out mistakes made in construction and helped his imitators perfect the appliance they had stolen from him.

Yes, such things do happen in daily life. They are happening every day. As we read of them or hear of them or meet people who are actors in such a drama, we are conscious of admiration for the deed, a quickening of the pulse, and the thankful thought that the world is not such a bad place after all.

But are we to stop with quickened heartbeats and gratitude for the greatness of heart shown by others? How about the bitterness we have been treasuring against some one who has injured us—or some one we think has injured us (it is astonishing how many of the slights and indignities for which vengeance has been vowed are only imaginary, after all!) How long do we intend to persist in treasuring the grudge that has perhaps already caused sorrow that cannot be measured? Let's be courageous enough to own ourselves in the wrong, when we are in the wrong, and to forgive the evil that has been kept alive by our persistent efforts to remember it. Let the quickened pulse-beat be ours not merely because we are hearing about forgiveness, but because we ourselves are rejoicing in friendship restored.

IV
FORGETTING WRONGS

There are people whose minds are like a lumber-room, littered with all sorts of odds and ends. In such a room it is impossible to count on laying hands promptly on a desired article, and in such a mind confusion takes the place of order. The mind had better be empty. An empty mind presents a fine opening for the proper kind of filling, but a confused mind is hopeless. How is it possible to make the memory a helpful servant unless nothing is allowed to find lodgment there that is not worth while?

An old proverb says, "No one can keep the birds from flying about his head, but one can keep them from nesting in his hair." That proverb points the way to saving the mind from becoming a lodging place for lumbering thoughts and ideas; everything that is certain to hinder instead of help one to be worth-while to the world must be told that there is "positively no admittance."

Among the things one must not afford permission to pass the bars is the thought that some associate may have said or done something that seemed like a slight or an injury. No man can afford to injure another, but any man can better afford to be injured than to allow his thoughts to dwell on the injury, to brood over it, until he is in a degree unfitted for his work. Far better is it to be like a father who said to his son when the latter, years after the commission of the deed, was speaking of his sorrow that he had grieved his father so: "Son, you must be dreaming; I don't recall the incident."

Then one must know when to forget evil things heard of another. Sometimes it is necessary to remember such facts, but so often the insinuations made concerning other people are not worth consideration, because they are not true. Even where there is ground for them, they are not proper subjects for thought and remembrance.

It is best to forget past achievements, unless they are made stepping-stones to greater achievements, spurs to work that could never be done without them. Yet how often the temptation comes to gloat in thought over these things, and over the good things said of one because of them, while opportunities for greater things are passed by. Thus a school-boy thought with delight of a word of commendation from his teacher when he ought to have been giving attention to the recitation of the pupil next to him; the result was a reprimand that stung. A soldier in the trenches has no time to gaze in admiration at the medal he has won by valor when at any moment there may sound the call to deeds of still greater valor. No more should a civilian imperil future success by failure to forget "the things which are behind."

The individual who refuses to forget a kindness he has done to someone else is another cumberer of the ground. A safe rule is, never forget a kindness received from another, but forget at once a kindness done to another. It is not difficult to sympathize with the youth who, after being reminded for the twentieth time by his brother of a trip to New Orleans for which the brother had paid out of his savings, said, "Yes, and I wish I had never taken a cent of the money!"

A thing to be forgotten always is the off-color story with which some people persist in polluting the atmosphere. Unfortunately there are always to be found folks like the young man of whom Donald Hankey said "He talks about things that I won't even think." When such talk is heard, don't think of it. If you do, you are apt to think of it again and again, until, perhaps, you will be telling it to some one else. And no one wants to be remembered as was the business man, proposed for the presidency of a great concern, of whom one said, "No, don't let's have him; he has earned a reputation for telling questionable stories."

If a good memory is to be a good servant, it must be trained to remember only the things that are helpful. And that takes courage!

V
GETTING RID OF EVIL

One of the trying disappointments of daily life comes with the discovery that something on which we have been depending is no longer worthy of confidence, because a foreign substance, some adulterant, has been mixed with it, without our knowledge. This seemed to be the case perhaps more than ever before during the recent days of war when a severe strain was put on the products of nearly every kind.

In many parts of the country those who were compelled to replenish their coal supply during the worst weather of a severe winter complained because the anthracite then secured gave out little heat; it contained such a large proportion of culm or other waste product which, in ordinary times, is carefully removed before shipment, that it could not do its work properly.

Disappointed in their anthracite, some turned to bituminous coal, only to find that at least fifty per cent, of a shipment received during the days of stress was made up of rock and clay.

Experience with the coal should have prepared one of the purchasers for his disappointment in a restaurant where he had been accustomed to be served with a splendid oyster stew. But he was surprised and displeased when he found that at least one-third of the milk which should have gone into the stew had been displaced by water.

At home that evening the same man was told more of the activity of dealers who permit impurities to interfere with the comfort of those who like pure products; the grocer had that day sent a package of soup beans which contained at least ten per cent. of gravel.

It is easy to appreciate the disappointment and embarrassment that come from the failure of the coal dealer, the restaurant keeper or the grocer to supply us with pure food and fuel. Then isn't it strange that we are apt to pay so little attention to the adulterants in character that are the cause of so much of the world's sorrow? That is to say, it seems odd that we pay so little attention to the things in our own lives that interfere; we are not apt to find it a difficult matter to rail at others because they permit evil to mix with good in their lives. Our vision is so much better when we are looking at motes in others than when we are looking straight past the beams in our own make-up.

There is daily need for each one of us to ask God for grace to go on a hunt for the evil that adulterates his own life, making it a disappointment to others and a cause of sorrow to God. Those who are bold enough to scrutinize themselves without flinching will be apt to find not merely things that are unquestionably evil, but they will be dismayed to see that even much of the good in which they have been taking comfort is adulterated with evil—as, for instance, the deed of helpfulness performed for a friend with the unconscious thought, "Some day he may be able to do something for me," or the gift made to a needy cause, accompanied by the assurance that the treasurer of the fund is one whom we particularly wish to impress with our liberality so that possibly a future benefit will come from him to us.

The adulterants of evil mixed with the good in our lives must be removed. And there is just one way to get rid of them—to submit ourselves to the sifting of Him who not only knows the good from the evil, the wheat from the chaff, but will also show the way to retain the wheat and throw out the chaff.

Of course one does not have to yield himself to Christ's sifting. But of one thing we can be sure; there will be a sifting. If Christ is not invited to do the work, the Devil will take up the task. But his purpose in sifting is always to retain the evil, and drive out all the good.

God asks for "pure religion and undefiled." There is no place in his calculations for adulterants. Be courageous, and get rid of them!

VI
LOOKING BEYOND MONEY

Money is a good thing, when it is properly secured and properly used. But there are better things than money. Honor is better, and loving service, and thoughtful consideration of others.

This was the lesson taught by the life of a man who was a shareholder in a mining company that was about to go out of business. The shareholders would sustain very heavy losses, so a friend who knew the secrets of the company determined to warn this man, whom everybody liked. The hint was given that it would be to his advantage to sell quickly. "Why?" asked Mr. N. "Well, you know, the value of the mines is greatly depreciated." "When I bought the shares I took the risk." "Yes, but now you should take the opportunity of selling while you can, so as not to lose anything." "And supposing I don't sell, what then?" "Then you will probably lose all you have." "And if I do sell, somebody else will lose instead of me?" "Yes, I suppose so." "Do you suppose Jesus Christ would sell out?" "That is hardly a fair question. I suppose he would not." "I am a Christian," said Mr. N., "and I wish to follow my Master, therefore I shall not sell." He did not, and soon after lost everything, and had to begin life again.

This shareholder would have appreciated Professor A. H. Buchanan, who was for forty years professor of mathematics in Cumberland University, Tennessee. After his death it was told of him that at one time he was offered an appointment in government service to which a $3,000 salary attached. His income as professor in a church college was $600 a year. But he saw more chance to make his life count for Christian things in the professor's place than in public service, so he declined the $3000 and stayed by the $600. One who spoke of these facts in the professor's life said, in comment:

"If he had taken the $3,000, everybody would have regarded him as an ordinary sort of man. Now everybody who has heard of Professor Buchanan's exceptional devotion appreciates that he was a very extraordinary man. A very cheap person indeed is capable of accepting a bigger salary."

At about the time of the death of this professor of mathematics a daily paper mentioned a civil engineer who was transforming the appearance of a western city, and said of him: "Two or three times he has had chances to get three or four times his present salary. Each time he has said: 'No, my work is here; I haven't finished it. The money doesn't count, so I shall stick here and finish my work.'"

After the death of a famous minister in St. Louis a story was told of him that he had not allowed to be known widely during his lifetime. This was the romantic tale, as related by a writer in The New York *Sun:*

"When a young man, he found to his amazement among his father's papers a deed to five thousand eight hundred and eighty-three acres of land, located in what is known as West Virginia. This deed was a great surprise to all who saw or heard of it. Putting this deed in his pocket, young Palmore, the only heir to the property, made a trip to West Virginia, to look over his vast estate, which was far in the interior.

"Starting from the city of Charleston, West Virginia, he drove in a buggy into the region where his plantation was located. He traced the boundaries of his property and found that hundreds of families had settled on it without any right to it, but were living as if secure in the possession of their separate little patches of territory. He found that beneath the surface of this land there was almost limitless wealth, but the multitudes who had built themselves humble homes on the surface did not know of it, and had been living thus in undisturbed possession for a number of years. He quietly walked about at night and looked through the windows at the parents and children living on his estate. Great lawyers were ready to inaugurate legal proceedings that would have made him a millionaire, and such legal proceedings would doubtless have been instituted if the heir in person had not visited the scene of his great estate. As he dreamed in the nighttime about dispossessing such a multitude of people of their humble homes, he began to feel that, instead of such a fortune being a blessing, an estate received at such an expense would be a burden.

"After earnest prayer and sleepless hours in the midst of his vast acres, he was seized with the conviction that each member of this multitude of families living on his property needed it more than did the heir, and there and then he made up his mind that he would leave them in quiet possession of his estate."

The reporter who related the story said that the man had been called a fool, and commented, "He was God's fool."

Then he said that the incident he had related would have been unbelievable if it had not been so well attested. But why unbelievable? Is it because of the common idea that "every man has his price," that it is unthinkable that a sane man would let a fortune that he could claim honestly slip through his fingers?

Perhaps it is true that every man has his price. However, if this snarl of the pessimist is to have universal application, the price must be understood to be—in many instances—not selfish gratification, but the opportunity for courageous service. There are men and women who can be won by such an opportunity who cannot be reached by any argument of mere private advantage. Such people silence the complaints of the croaker and command the confidence of those who are struggling to help their fellows.

Louis Agassiz, the naturalist, was such a man. "I have no time to make money," was his remark when urged by a friend to turn aside from the important work of the moment to an easy, lucrative task. His reason was thus explained at another time: "I have made it the rule of my life to abandon any intellectual pursuit the moment it becomes commercially valuable." It was his idea that there were many who would then be willing to carry on work he had begun.

A contrast is presented by the famous inventor who, early in life, made it a rule never to give himself to any activity in which there was no prospect of financial gain. His first question was not, "Does the public need this invention?" but "Is there money in it?" Having answered to his satisfaction, he was ready to go ahead.

The world could not well have spared either of these men, for both rendered valuable service. But, judging from the stories of their careers, there was more joy in the life of the naturalist, who, satisfied to earn a living, thought most of serving his fellows, than in the life of the inventor before whose eyes the dollar continually loomed large. The counting-house measure of life is not the most satisfying nor is it the most useful.

That was the notion of Jacob Riis, of whom a minister who was devoting his life to the interest of young working men near his church once asked if such effort was merely thrown away, if he was pocketing himself. "Pocketing yourself, are you?" Riis replied. "Stick to your pocket. It is a pretty good pocket to be in. Out of such a pocket, worked in the way you are working it, will come healing for the ills of the day that now possess us. I would rather be in such a pocket, working for the Lord, than in a $1,000,000 church, working for the applause of a congregation."

Those who are familiar with inside history at Washington say that the day after Garfield's election as President, a dispatch was sent to Milton Wells, a Wisconsin preacher, whose vote in the convention had kept Garfield's name on the list of candidates to the very last, asking him if he would become governor of Arizona Territory. Mr. Wells answered: "I have a better office that I cannot leave. I am preaching here for $600 per year."

There was once a man named Paul who might have enjoyed position and power, if he had wished, but he chose instead a life of courageous service of which he was able once to write, without boasting:

"In labors more abundantly, in prisons more abundantly; in stripes above measure, in deaths oft. Of the Jews five times received I forty stripes save one. Thrice was I beaten with rods, once was I stoned, thrice I suffered shipwreck, a night and a day have I been in the deep; in journeyings often, in perils of rivers, in perils of robbers, in perils from my countrymen, in perils from the Gentiles, in perils in the city, in perils in the wilderness, in perils in the sea, in perils among false brethren; in labor and travail, in watchings often, in hunger and thirst, in fastings often, in cold and nakedness."

How could Paul bear all these things? They were enough to break down a dozen strong men. Probably he sometimes felt that he could not bear the burden any longer, but always there came to him the assurance of Christ, "My grace is sufficient for thee." Then he could bear anything; yet not he, but Christ, who lived in him. Thus his glory was not in his own strength but in his weakness, which made place in his life for the strength of Christ.

Until men and women learn how to gain strength in their weakness as Paul did, their lives will be unsatisfying, their days will be full of complaint. Their burdens, which seemed like mountains before learning to trust Christ, will be borne as easily as if they were feathers.

God does not promise to make us all dollar millionaires if we look at Him for strength in our weakness, but He does promise to make us all millionaires of faith and hope and courage. Paul was; we can be, too.

"YOU may expect to spend the rest of your days tied to your chair."

Theodore Roosevelt's physician made this disconcerting announcement to his patient a few weeks before his death.

How would the courageous man receive an announcement like that? How would you receive it?

Let the words spoken in reply by the lion-hearted Roosevelt never be forgotten by others who struggle with difficulties:

"All right! I can work and live that way, too!"

Surely the triumphant words justified the characterization made by Herman Hagedorn of this colossal worker:

"He was frail; he made himself a mountain of courage."

At a dinner given to celebrate the worthy achievement of a public man, a guest spoke of him to a companion at table.

"No wonder he has been so well. Everything is in his favor: he is young, he is brilliant, he is in good health."

"In good health?" was the answering comment. "Where did you get that? For years he has been in wretched health; many a night he was unable to sleep except he knelt on the floor by the bedside and stretched himself from his waist across the bed. But it is not strange that you did not know, he has said nothing of his ailments; he is so full of courage himself that he makes everyone around him courageous."

I
LEARNING

When the famous Sioux Indian, Charles A. Eastman, was a boy, his father, who had learned the joys of civilized life, urged his son to secure an education. "I am glad that my son is brave and strong," he said to him. "I have come to start you on the White Man's way. I want you to grow to be a good man."

Then he urged his son, Ohiyesa, as he was called, to put on the civilized clothes he had brought with him. The boy rebelled at first; he had been accustomed to hate white men and everything that belonged to them. But when he reflected that they had done him no harm, after all, he decided to try on the curious garments.

Together father and son traveled toward the haunts of the white man. As they traveled Ohiyesa listened to tales of the wonderful inventions he would see. He was especially eager to look on a railroad train.

But even after he had gone with his father, he was reluctant to enter on his long training, until his father suggested that he make believe he was starting on a long war-path, from which there could be no honorable return until his course was completed. Entering into the spirit of the proposal, the Indian lad began his schooling at Flandreau Indian Agency, and persisted for twelve long years. After graduating from college he devoted himself to his people, and in many years since has accomplished wonders for them, teaching them the patience he had himself learned, and enabling them to understand that such patience and persistence always brings its reward.

The experience of Isaac Pitman, the inventor of shorthand, was different, yet, after all, it was much the same. As a boy he had little education. But soon after he went to work he made up his mind to supply the lack. The record of how he did this is one of the most remarkable instances of courageous patience on record.

The long office hours at his place of employment, from six in the morning until six at night, made study difficult, but he showed conclusively that where there is a will there is a way, and that he had the will. He was accustomed to leave his bed at four, that he might study two hours before the beginning of the day's work. Two hours in the evening also were set apart for study. Sometimes it happened that work at the factory was light, and the young clerk was excused for the morning. Instead of taking the time for sport, it was his habit to take a book with him into the fields or under the trees.

Thomas Allen Reid, in his biography of Pitman says: "One of the books which he made his companion in morning walks into the country was Lennie's Grammar. The conjugation of verbs, list of irregular verbs, adverbs, prepositions, and conjunctions, and the thirty-six rules of syntax, he committed to memory so that he could repeat them in order. The study of the books gave him a transparent English style."

His father was a subscriber to the local library. "I went regularly to the library for fresh supplies of books," Isaac said, in 1863, "and thus read most of the English classics. I think I was quite as familiar with Addison, and Sir Roger, and Will Honeycomb, and all the Club, as I was with my own brothers and sisters . . . and when reading The Spectator at that early age, I wished that I might be able to do something in letters."

Before he left school he formed the habit of copying choice pieces of poetry and prose into a little book which he kept in his pocket. These bits he would commit to memory when he had leisure. A later pocket companion contained a neatly written copy of Valpey's Greek Grammar, as far as the syntax, which he committed to memory. In his morning walks in 1832 he committed to memory the first fourteen chapters of Proverbs. He would not undertake a fresh chapter until he had repeated the preceding one without hesitation.

As most of his knowledge of words was gained from books, he had difficulty in pronunciation. "His method of overcoming the deficiency was ingenious," his biographer wrote. "Again and again he read 'Paradise Lost.' Careful attention to the meter enabled him to correct his faulty pronunciation of many words. Words not found in the poem he discovered in the dictionary. With unusual courage he decided to read through Walker's Dictionary, fixing his mind on words new to him and on the spelling and pronunciation of familiar terms. On the pages of one of his pocket-books he copied all words he had been in the habit of mispronouncing. Although there were more than two thousand of these words, the plan was carried out before he was seventeen."

The labor of writing out so many extracts from books led him to study the imperfect system of shorthand then current, and to develop the system that was to bear his name.

So many young people feel that they "simply cannot abide" the long process of getting an education; they give up when they are only a part of the way to the goal. But for most of them the day of bitter regret will come when they will wish that they had been more like Eastman or Pitman in their determination to be patient and persistent, to allow nothing to stand in the way of their purpose to fit themselves in the best possible manner for the serious business of life.

II
DEPENDING ON SELF

Young men just starting out in life nowadays, who find the path to success difficult, are more fortunate than some of those who struggled with hard times a century or more ago, because they are determined to make a self-respecting fight on their own merits. It was not always so; once nothing was thought of the effort made by an impecunious young man to throw himself on the generosity of one who had already achieved success. Then it was a habit of many authors to seek as a patron a man of influence and means who would help them live till their books were ready for the publisher, and then help to get the books before the public.

From letters of George Crabbe, a poet of some note in his century, asking Edmund Burke to become his patron, something of his story may be known. As a boy he was apprenticed to an apothecary; later he was proprietor of a small shop of his own. Business, neglected for books and writing, did not prosper. With his sister, his housekeeper, he "fasted with much fortitude." Then he went to London, with a capital of nine pounds, and starved some more. Months were spent in trying to enlist two patrons. At last, threatened with a prison for debt, he decided to try a third patron; and this was his procedure, as he himself described it:

"I looked as well as I could into every character that offered itself to my view, and resolved to apply where I found the most shining abilities, for I had learnt to distrust the humanity of weak people in all stations."

So he wrote to Edmund Burke, telling him that he could no longer be content to live in the home of poor people, who had kept him for nearly a year, and had lent him money for his current expenses. Describing himself as "one of those outcasts on the world, who are without a friend, without employment and without bread," he told of his vain appeal to another for gold to save him from prison, added that he had but one week to raise the necessary funds, and made his request.

"I appeal to you, sir, as a good, and, let me add, a great man. I have no other pretensions to your favor than that I am an unhappy one. It is not easy to support thoughts of confinement, and I am coward enough to dread such an end to my suspense . . . I will call upon you, sir, to-morrow, and if I have not the happiness to obtain credit with you I must submit to my fate . . . I have only to hope a speedy end to a life so unpromisingly begun . . . I can reap some consolation in looking to the end of it."

The appeal was successful. Edmund Burke became Crabbe's patron. The poet was glad to eat the crumbs that fell from the rich man's table, and submitted to many unpleasant slights and insinuations while he received the dole of charity.

That suing thus for a patron did not always have the effect of destroying an author's self-respect is shown by a letter written by Dr. Samuel Johnson to Lord Chesterfield. When, after years of hard labor, Dr. Johnson's dictionary was known to be ready for publication, Lord Chesterfield wrote for "The World" two flattering articles about the author, evidently thinking that the work would be dedicated to him. At once Dr. Johnson wrote:

"My Lord: When, upon some slight encouragement, I first visited your lordship, I . . . could not forbear to wish . . . that I might obtain that regard for which I saw the world contending; but I found my attendance so little encouraged, that neither pride nor modesty would suffer me to continue it. . . .

"Seven years, my lord, have passed since I waited in your outward room, or was repulsed from your door, during which time I have been pushing on my work through difficulties, of which it is useless to complain, and have brought it at last to the verge of publication, without one act of assistance, one word of encouragement or one smile of favor. Such treatment I did not expect for I never had a patron before. . . . The notice which you have been pleased to take of my labor, had it been early, had been kind; but it has been delayed till I am indifferent, and cannot enjoy it; till I am solitary, and cannot impart it; till I am known, and do not want it. . . . I have long awakened from that dream of hope, in which I once boasted myself with so much exultation, my lord,

"Your lordship's most humble, most obedient servant,

"Sam Johnson."

The lapse of a century has brought a change. Self-respecting, courageous young workers do not seek a patron to help them to fame. To-day they ask only to fight their own battles, win their own victories.

III
UNCOMPLAINING

Nor do courageous workers complain when little things go wrong.

"I don't know what I shall do if the mail does not come to-morrow. Think of being two days without a morning paper!"

The complaint was heard when railway traffic had been tied up by washouts on the railway. The inconvenience suffered by the speaker seemed to him very great. Though there had been no other interruption to the many comforts and conveniences to which he had been accustomed, the single difficulty made him lose his temper and spoiled his day.

When one is tempted to magnify such a small difficulty into a mountain it is worth while to look at things from the standpoint of a man whose life far from the centers of civilization makes him so independent of circumstances and surroundings that he can be cheerful even in the face of what seem like bitter privations.

A company of travelers in the forests of Canada thought that the knowledge of the most recent news was necessary to happiness. They learned their mistake when they reached the camp of a man from whom they expected to learn news more recent than the events reported in the paper the day they left civilization, seven weeks before. They felt sure that, as he lived on the trail, he would have seen some traveler who had left the railroad since their own departure.

When they asked him for late news from the States, he said he had some very recent news, and proceeded to tell of events eight months old! "Do you call that recent?" he was asked, in disgust.

"What's the matter with that?" was the wondering reply. "It only happened last fall, and there ain't been nobody through here since." And he contentedly resumed the task at which he had been engaged when interrupted by the demand for "recent" news.

On the same journey the travelers—whose story is told in "Trails in Western Canada"—showed that they were learning the lesson. Carelessness in handling a campfire caused a forest fire which threatened their food supply. They saved this, but lost their only axes. After a long search they found these in the embers, but the temper had been utterly ruined by the heat. Only a few hours before they felt that an axe was absolutely necessary not only to comfort but to life itself, yet when the ruined tools were found the travelers turned to their tasks without giving the disaster a second thought. They knew that there is always a way out of difficulty. They continued their expedition without an axe, and found that they managed very well.

The lesson was impressed still more by the attitude of a guide who spent a few days with them. Like many other people on vacation they allowed themselves to worry about finances. But their thoughts were set on a new track by the guide, who, after telling of the success in trapping grizzly bear and beaver which had enabled him to save a little money, said: "Life is too short to worry about money. If I lose all I have to-morrow, I can get a couple of bear traps and by next spring I'll be on my feet again. The mountains are always here, and I know where there is a bunch of bear and a colony of beaver, and I can get along out here, and live like a prince while those poor millionaires are lying awake at nights, lest someone come and steal their money."

Two other guides were engaged to pole the travelers' raft down the Fraser River. Nearly every day the cold rain fell in torrents, but the men were unmoved. "All day long they would stand in their wet clothes, their hands numb and blue from the cold as they handled their dripping poles; yet not a comment indicating discomfort is recalled. Physical annoyances, which in the city would bring an ambulance, scarcely are mentioned by them."

One day one of the men was asked what they did when they were sick. "Cain't say we ever are sick," was the reply. "The worst thing that ever happened to us, I reckon, was when Mort here had a bad tooth; but, after a day or two, we got sick of it, and took it out." That was all he thought worth saying about it till he was pressed for an account of the operation. "Oh, I looked through our dunnage bag," he said, "and found an old railroad spike. Mort held it against the tooth and I hit the head with a big rock, and knocked her out the first time."

His companion was unwilling to agree that this was the most trying experience. He told of a day when the man who had reported the tooth extraction, cut his foot severely with an axe. "Oh, that didn't bother us," the victim interrupted. "I just slapped on some spruce gum and never thought anything more about it." Asked how long he was laid up, the surprised answer was: "Laid up for that? We weren't laid up at all. Couldn't travel quite as fast for a day or two, but we didn't lose no time at that, for we traveled longer to make up."

Still another guide gave an object lesson in making light of difficulties when his horse fell on him, bruising one of his knees so that it swelled to an enormous size. The injured man made no complaint, though his companions were full of sympathy. He knew he could reduce the swelling by heroic remedies.

One day when traveling was unusually difficult, the guide cheered his employers by telling them of the fine camp he owned just ahead—"a house like a hotel," he said. And when the camp was reached he pointed proudly to "a great log with a few great pieces of bark and some cedar slivers stretched over the top." In this camp the night was spent, without blankets and in the rain. "But as no one seemed to consider this anything out of the ordinary, the travelers made no complaint."

Perhaps a taste of the wilderness is what we need when we become impatient of trifles and make ourselves miserable because everything does not go to suit us.

IV
PERSISTING

Failure camps on the trail of the man who is ready to give up because difficulties multiply. A representative of a large paper warehouse made up his mind to add to his list of customers a certain Michigan firm. Repeated rebuffs did not daunt him. Every sixty days he sent the firm a letter of invitation to buy his goods. During twenty-seven years one hundred and sixty-one letters were mailed without result. Then, in reply to the one hundred and sixty-second letter, the Michigan firm asked for quotations. These were given promptly, and two carloads of paper were sold. What if this letter writer had become discouraged before he wrote this final letter?

"I thought you were planning to complete your education," a friend said to a young man whom he had not seen for some time; "yet now you are clerking in a store. Perhaps, though, you are earning money for next year's expenses."

"No, I am earning money for this year's expenses," was the discouraged reply. "I did want an education, but I found it was too difficult to get what I sought, so I have decided to settle down."

Of course it is easier to give up than it is to push on in the face of difficulty, but the youth who pushes on is fitting himself to fill a man's place in the world, while the young man who is easily discouraged is fitting himself for nothing but disappointment. The world has no place for a quitter.

There is a tonic for young people who purpose to make the most of themselves in glimpses of a few college students who had the courage to face difficulty. One of these was an Italian boy, who was glad to beat carpets, wash windows, scrub kitchen floors, mow lawns, teach grammar, arithmetic and vocal exercises at a night school for foreigners. Then—as if his time was not fully occupied by these occupations—he made arrangements to care for a furnace and sift the ashes, in exchange for piano lessons. That student finished his preparatory course with credit, taking a prize for scholarship.

A seventeen-year-old boy wanted an education, but he had nine brothers and sisters at home, and he knew that he could look for no financial assistance from his parents. So he picked cotton at sixty cents a hundred pounds, sawed wood, cut weeds and scrubbed floors—and thus paid his expenses.

One student could not spare the money to pay his railroad fare to the school of his choice. But he had a pony. So he rode the pony the entire distance of five hundred miles, working for his expenses along the way.

A beginner in college was too full of grit to give up when bills came on him more heavily than he had expected. During the school year he did chores, rang the bell for the change of classes, did janitor work, and waited on table in restaurants. In the summer he found work on farms near by.

"No task is too difficult for the man with a purpose," declared a worker with young men, some of whom were ready to give up. "Two things are necessary if you would be successful," was another man's message to those whom he wished to inspire to do purposeful work. "First: know what you want to do. Second: do it."

Those who permit obstacles to stand in the way of the performance of tasks they know they ought to perform if they would make the most of themselves, need to take to heart the message given by a mother to her son when he was ready to give up the unequal struggle with poverty and physical infirmity. "Thou wilt have much to bear, many hardships to suffer," she said. "But mark what I say, we must not mind the trouble. During the first part of the night we must prepare the bed on which to stretch ourselves during the latter part."

Giving up after failure is always easier than trying again, but the men and women who count are those who will not be dismayed by failure. When J. Marion Sims, the famous surgeon, was beginning the practice of medicine, he proudly tacked an immense tin sign on the front of his office. Then he lost two patients, and pride and courage both failed him. "I just took down that long tin signboard from my door," he wrote in the story of his life. "There was an old well back of the house, covered over with boards. I went to the well, took that sign with me, dropped it in there, and covered the old well over again. I was no longer a doctor in the town." But fortunately he conquered discouragement, made a fresh beginning, and overcame tremendous obstacles. After his death a famous man said that if all his discoveries should be suppressed, it would be found that his own peculiar branch of surgery had gone backward at least twenty-five years.

Indomitable perseverance is necessary for the business man as for the professional man; and it will just as surely bring reward to those who are engaged in Christian work as to those who are seeking worldly honor. So when the uphill climb seems too difficult, there must be no faltering. Remember—as Christina Rossetti said—"We shall escape the uphill by never turning back."

In gathering material for a history of Charles V of Spain, a Spanish historian was painstaking in his researches. Finally he was able to tell the king's whereabouts on every day of his career, except for two weeks in 1538.

Then friends assured him that he had done his best. In all probability nothing of importance happened during those days. But the historian believed in being thorough to the end. So he delayed publication. For fifteen years he sought news of the missing fortnight. Finally, and reluctantly, when he was seventy-five years old, he published the book.

At length an American woman, studying in the archives of Spain, having learned of the lost days, resolved to find them. Among musty documents, in many libraries, she toiled. Then, by a woman's intuition, she was led to look for documents of a sort the Spanish historian had never thought of. And she found where the king was on some of those days. The news was sent to the historian, just in time for him to make additions to his inaugural address to be delivered on taking his seat in the Academy of History. In this address he rejoiced to give full credit for the discovery to the American.

But the woman was not satisfied; there was still a gap to be filled. She made further trials, and failed. Again intuition led her to documentary sources that had hardly been touched since they were filed away nearly three hundred years before. She succeeded, and now that bit of history is complete.

A well known writer for young people was also persistent in tracing a story to its source. When he came to America from his native Holland he heard for the first time the story of the Dutch hero who stopped the hole in the dike, a story unknown in Holland. He resolved to prove or disprove this. The record of his long search was published later. Not only did he prove the existence of the boy, but he proved that the boy's sister was a partner in the heroic deed. Thus the helpful story has been saved for future generations.

These incidents make interesting reading. But do they not do more? Surely it is unnecessary to urge the lesson of persistence in a task seriously undertaken. Often there is temptation to slight some worth-while task, after one has worked on it painstakingly for a time. "Why pay so much attention to detail?" is asked. "Surely no real harm will be done if I give less time to some of these things that seemed so important at the beginning!"

Fortunately there are multitudes of workers who are constitutionally unable to slight a task. The proofreader on a paper of large circulation is an example. It is a part of her work to prove statements made, to verify facts and figures, to see that these are altogether accurate. Once when there was an unusual pressure of work the editor suggested that she might wish to take certain things for granted, but she showed her conscientious thoroughness by performing the task to the end, according to the rules of the office, and in the face of weariness that was almost exhaustion.

It may not be given to you to be a historian. You may not be called upon to prove the story of a hero. It may not be your task to read proof or to verify manuscripts. But each one has a definite part in the work of the world and there is no one to whom the example of historian and proofreader is without value. All need to remember the truth in the assurance, "There is nothing so hard but search will find it out."

V
TOILING

Two young people were passing out of a building where they had just listened to a speaker of note.

"What a wonderful talk that was!" said one who found it a heavy cross to make the simplest address in public. "I wish I had such a gift of speech."

"It isn't a gift in his case; it is an acquirement," was the response. "If you had known that man five years ago, you would agree with me. When I first knew him he could not get up in a public meeting and make the simplest statement without floundering and stammering in a most pitiful manner. But he had made up his mind to be a public speaker, and he put himself through a severe course of discipline. To-day you see the result."

The biography of Dr. Herrick Johnson tells of courageous conquest of difficulties that seemed to block the way to success: "Hamilton College has always given great attention to public speaking and class orations. The high standard was set by a remarkably gifted man, Professor Mandeville, who instituted a system in the study of oratory and public speaking which has been known ever since, with some modification, as the 'Mandeville System.'"

"In 1853, Dr. Anson J. Upson was in the Mandevillian chair, and had lifted up to still greater height the standard of public speaking, and had awakened a great, inextinguishable enthusiasm for it. Not one of the boys who entered that year, and who were at that prize-speaking contest, could fail to be seized with the public-speaking craze. It especially met Herrick Johnson's taste and trend and gifts, and fired his highest aim. Probably there was nothing he wanted so much as the prize in his class at the next commencement. But unfortunately his standards and ideals of public speaking were just then as far as possible from the Mandevillian standard. He had acquired what was called a ministerial tone, and other faults fatal to any success, unless eradicated. The best speakers of the upper classes were the recognized and accepted 'drillers' of the new boys, who at once put themselves under their care and criticism. Every spring and fall a certain valley with a grove, north of the college, was the resort of the aspirants for success at this time. The woods would ring with their 'exercises' and strenuous declamation, and I presume it is the same to-day.

"Herrick Johnson had a magnificent voice, well-nigh ruined by his sins against the right method of using it. He soon saw that it was going to be essential for him to go down to the foundation of his wrong methods and break them all up and absolutely eradicate his 'tone.' It was no easy thing to do, but the young man was intensely ambitious, and so he worked with the greatest energy. He failed of an appointment on the 'best four' of his Freshman class. But he worked away throughout his Sophomore year and failed again. The upperclassmen saw his pluck, they recognized his grand voice, and they worked with him during his Junior year, until he had mastered the Mandevillian style, wholly eradicated his 'tone,' corrected all defects, and got his appointment for one of the best four speakers of the Junior year; and on the prize-speaking night of that commencement, he went on the platform conscious of his power and swept everything before him as the Junior prize speaker. It set the standard for that young man. Voice, manner, address, were all masterful and accounted easily for his great success as a public speaker through all his subsequent prominent and successful career in his profession."

A part of the good of "speaking a piece" is to try again, determined to retrieve failure. Success is not always a good thing for a boy or a girl, any more than for a man or a woman. The discipline of failure is sometimes needed. To fail is not always a calamity, if the failure leads to the correction of the faults that lead to failure. Whether it be speaking a piece or learning a lesson or facing a trying situation in business, no matter how many times one has failed, he needs to take to heart the message of Macbeth:

We fail!
But screw your courage to the sticking-point,
And we'll not fail.

Always there is a reward for those who fight against difficulties, who persist in their struggle even when failure follows failure. Everyday the glad story of the sequel to such persistent struggles is recorded. The records of commercial life, of school life, of home life are full of these.

VI
CONQUERING INFIRMITY

Of all obstacles that can stand in the way of courageous conquest, one of the most fatal, in the opinion of many, is blindness. Yet it is not necessary that the loss of the eyes should be the fatal handicap it is almost universally considered. It is a mistake to feel that when a worker has anything seriously and permanently wrong with his eyes he cannot be expected longer to perform tasks that are normal for one who has the full use of all his five senses. In fact, when we hear that a man is going blind we are apt to dismiss with a sigh his chance for continuing productive labor of any sort; we feel that there is little left for him but sitting resignedly in a chimney corner and listening to others read to him or patiently fingering the raised letters provided for the use of the blind.

In protest against this error a novelist has taken for his hero a young man who lost his sight. His friends pitied him, talked dolefully to him, promised to look after him in the days of incapacity. Of course he sank lower and lower in the doleful dumps. Then one came into his life who never seemed to notice his blindness, who talked to him as if he could see, who encouraged him to do things by taking it for granted that they would be performed. Her treatment proved effective; before long the blind man was learning self-reliance, and was well on the road to achievement.

The story was true to life for, times without number, blind men and women have shown their ability to work as effectively as if they could see. More than two hundred years ago a teacher in London named Richard Lucas lost his eyesight. Many of his friends thought that he would, of course, give up all idea of being a useful man; in that day few thought of the possibility of one so afflicted doing anything worth much. But the young man thought differently. He listened to others as they read to him, and completed his studies. He became the author of a dozen volumes, and was among the leaders of his day. One of his greatest works was the book "An Enquiry after Happiness." He knew how to be happy, in spite of his affliction, so he could teach others to follow him.

A little earlier there lived on the farm of a poor Irishman the boy Thomas Carolan. When he was five years old, he had smallpox, a disease that was much more virulent in those days than it is to-day because the treatment required was not understood. As a result the boy lost his sight. Soon he showed a taste for music, and he was able to take a few lessons, in spite of the poverty at home. As a young man he composed hundreds of pieces of music, and it has been said of him that he contributed much towards correcting and enriching the style of national Irish music.

Another youthful victim of smallpox was Thomas Blacklock, the son of a bricklayer in Scotland. "He can't be an artisan now," his friends said. But it did not occur to them that he could be a professional man. His father read him poetry and essays. When he was only twelve the boy began to write poetry in imitation of those whose verses he had heard. After his father's death, when the blind boy was but nineteen, he was more than ever dependent on himself. By the help of a friend he was enabled to go to school for a time. Then he became an author, and, later, a famous preacher. Often, as he walked about, a favorite dog preceded him. On one occasion he heard the hollow sound of the dog's tread on the board covering a deep well, and just in time to avoid stepping on the board himself. The covering was so rotten that he would surely have fallen into the water.

As a boy Francis Huber, of Geneva, Switzerland, was a great student. He insisted on reading by the feeble light of a lamp, or by the light of the moon, even when he was urged not to do so, and the result was blindness. A few years later he married one who rejoiced to be "his companion, his secretary and his observer." He became the greatest authority of his day on bees, although he knew nothing of the subject until after his misfortune. The strange thing is that all his conclusions were based on observation. Among other things he studied the function of the wax, the construction of their combs, the bees' senses and their ability to ventilate the hive by means of their wings. In recognition of his work he was given membership in a number of learned societies. His name must always be connected with the history of early bee investigation.

Not long after the close of the American Revolution James Holman, a British naval officer, lost his eyesight while in Africa. He was then about twenty-five years old. Later he became one of the best known travelers of his day. The world was told of his travels in lectures and in books, and others were also inspired to travel. "What is the use of traveling to one who cannot see?" he was asked at one time. "Does every traveler see all he describes?" he replied. He said that he felt sure he visited, when on his travels, as many interesting places as others, and that, by having the things described to him on the spot, he could form as correct a judgment as his own sight would have enabled him to do.

In 1779 Richmond, Virginia, gave birth to James Wilson, who lost his sight when he was four years old, because of smallpox. He was then on shipboard, and was taken to Belfast, Ireland, where he grew to manhood. When a boy he delivered newspapers to subscribers who lived as far as five miles from the city. When fifteen he used part of his earnings to buy books which he persuaded other boys to read to him. At twenty-one he entered an institution for the blind, for fuller instruction. Then he joined with a circle of mechanics in forming a reading society. One friend promised to read to him every evening such books as he could procure. The hours for reading were from nine to one every night in summer and from seven to eleven every night in the winter. "Often I have traveled three or four miles, in a severe winter night, to be at my post in time," he said once. "Perished with cold and drenched with rain, I have many a time sat down and listened for several hours together to the writings of Plutarch, Rollins, or Clarendon." After seven or eight years of this training, he was "acquainted with almost every work in the English language" his biographer says, perhaps a little extravagantly. His education he used in literary work.

B. B. Bowen was a Massachusetts boy just a century ago. When a babe he lost his sight. In 1833 Dr. Howe—husband of Julia Ward Howe—selected him as one of six blind boys on whom he was to make the first experiments in the instruction of the blind. Later he wrote a book of which eighteen thousand copies were sold.

Another of the men who proved the loss of sight was not a bar to successful work was Thomas R. Lounsbury, the Yale scholar whose studies in Chaucer and Shakespeare made him famous. Toward the close of his busy life he was engaged in a critical study of Tennyson, preparatory to writing an exhaustive book on the life of the great poet. He did not live to complete the work, but he left it in such shape that a friend was able to put it in the hands of the publishers.

In the Introduction to the biography this friend told of the courageous manner in which Professor Lounsbury faced threatening blindness and continued his writing in spite of the danger. We are told that his eyes, never very good, failed him for close and prolonged work. "At best he could depend upon them for no more than two or three hours a day. Sometimes he could not depend upon them at all. That he might not subject them to undue strain, he acquired the habit of writing in the dark. Night after night, using a pencil on coarse paper, he would sketch a series of paragraphs for consideration in the morning. This was almost invariably his custom in later years. Needless to say, these rough drafts are difficult reading for an outsider. Though the lines could be kept reasonably straight, it was impossible for a man enveloped in darkness to dot an *i* or to cross a *t*. Moreover, many words were abbreviated, and numerous sentences were left half written out. Every detail, however, was perfectly plain to the author himself. With these detached slips of paper and voluminous notes before him, he composed on a typewriter his various chapters, putting the paragraphs in logical sequence."

Francis Parkman, the historian who made the Indian wars real to fascinated readers, was a physical wreck on the completion of "The Oregon Trail," when he was but twenty-five years old. He could not write even his own name, except with his eyes closed; he was unable to fix his mind on a subject, except for very brief intervals, and his nervous system was so exhausted that any effort was a burden. But he would not give up. During the weary days of darkness he thought out the story of the conspiracy of Pontiac and decided to write it. Physicians warned him that the results would be disastrous, yet he felt that nothing could do him more harm than an idle, purposeless life.

One of his chief difficulties he solved in an ingenious manner. In a manuscript, published after his death, his plan was described:

"He caused a wooden frame to be constructed of the size and shape of a sheet of letter paper. Stout wires were fixed horizontally across it, half an inch apart, movable back of thick pasteboard fitted behind them. The paper for writing was placed between the pasteboard and wires, guided by which and using a black-lead crayon, he could write not illegibly with closed eyes."

This contrivance, with improvements, he used for about forty years of semi-blindness.

The documents on which he depended for his facts were read to him, though sometimes for days he could not listen, and then perhaps only for half an hour at a time. As he listened to the reading he made notes with closed eyes. Then he turned over in his mind what he had heard and laboriously wrote a few lines. For months he penned an average of only three or four lines a day. Later he was able to work more rapidly and he completed the book in two years and a half. No publisher was found who was willing to bear the expense of issuing the volume, and the young man paid for the plates himself.

Friends thought that now he would have to give up. His eyes were still troubling him, he became lame, his head felt as if great bands of iron were fastened about it, and frequently he did not sleep more than an hour or two a night. Then came the death of his wife, on whom he had depended for some years. At one time his physician warned him that he had not more than six months to live. But when a friend said that he had nothing more to live for, he made the man understand that he was not ready to hoist the white flag.

He lived for forty-five years after it was thought that he could never use his eyes again, and during all this time he worked steadily and patiently, accomplishing what would have been a large task for a man who had the full use of all his powers.

An Englishman was told by his physician he could never see again. For a time the news weighed heavily upon him. Afterward he said: "I remained silent for a moment, thinking seriously, and then, summoning up all the grit I possessed, I said, 'If God wills it, He knows best. What must be will be. And,' I added, putting my hand up to a tear that trickled down my face, 'God helping me, this is the last tear I shall ever shed for my blindness.'" It was. He secured the degrees of doctor of philosophy and master of arts. He was a fellow of the Royal Geographical Society and the Chemical Society. He made many valuable scientific discoveries and inventions, saved a millionaire's life, and received the largest fee ever awarded any doctor—$250,000.

To these men difficulties were a challenge to courage. They accepted the challenge and proved themselves superior to circumstances. Thus their lives became a challenge to the millions of their countrymen who read of their triumph.

CHAPTER THREE

THE COURAGE OF INDUSTRY

ANYBODY can drift, but only the man or woman of courage can breast the current, can fight on upstream.

It is so easy to be idle or to work listlessly. Average folks drift heedlessly into occupations in which they have no special interest and for which they have as little fitness. Most people waste their evenings or use them to little profit: it never occurs to them that each day they waste precious hours. They give more thought to schemes to do less work than to attempts to increase output.

And so they show their weakness, their unfitness for bearing responsibility, their cowardice when the world is calling for courage.

Worth-while work demands the finest kind of courage, and with perfect fairness work gives back courage to those who put courage into it.

I
BEGINNING

"Yes, he's a right good worker, when you once get him started," a country newspaper editor said to a friend who was inquiring about a boy who had been in the office three months. "Watch him now; you'll see what I mean."

The boy had just brought from the express office the package of "patent insides," as the papers for the weekly edition of the newspaper, already half printed in the nearby city, were called. With a sigh he dragged these up the stairs and laid them on the folding table. With another sigh he contemplated the pile and thought how much time would be required to fold the eight hundred papers. After lengthy calculation he stopped to read a column of jokes from the top paper in the pile. At least five minutes passed before the first paper was folded. At the end of ten minutes he had succeeded in folding perhaps twenty-five papers. When the noon hour arrived not one third of the task was completed.

While he ate his lunch he was thinking of the dread ordeal of the afternoon—six hundred more papers to be folded! Would he ever be done? He was still pitying himself as he walked slowly back to the office. Just before reaching the doorway into which he must turn, he spied an acquaintance. He made his way over to the boy who had attracted him, not because he had anything to say to him, but that he might delay a little longer the moment of beginning work at the folding table.

"What are you going to do?" he asked idly of the boy, who had taken off his coat and was rolling up his sleeves.

"The boss wants me to sort that lot of old iron," was the reply.

"What, that huge pile! It will take you a week, won't it? Just think how much of it there is!"

"No, there isn't time to think how much of it there is," was the reply. "And what would be the good? Not a bit of use getting discouraged at the very start, and that is what would happen if I didn't pitch in hard. The job is going to be done before night—that is, if I'm not interrupted by too many loafers coming in to ask fool questions."

The boy from the printing office was about to resent this speech of the boy at the iron pile, but he thought better of it. "Perhaps there is something in what he says," he said to himself, as he went up the stairs. "Suppose I try to pitch in hard."

So he surprised the foreman by beginning at the pile of six hundred papers as if he was to be sent to a ball game when he finished. And he surprised himself by finishing his task in a little more than an hour.

The lesson he learned that day stood him in good stead when later he was taking his first difficult examination in a technical school. His neighbor stopped to look over the paper from beginning to end, and was heard to mutter, "How do they expect us to get through ten questions like these in an hour's time?" The boy from the printing office had no time for such an inquiry, but began work at once on the first question, without troubling himself about those that came later until he was ready for them.

So it was when, his technical course completed, he was confronted by his first great railroad task, the clearing up of a wreck that looked to his assistants like an inextricable tangle. After one good look at it he pitched in for all he was worth, thus inspiring the men who had felt the task was impossible, and within a few hours the tracks were clear.

The ability to pitch in at once on a hard job is one characteristic of the man who accomplishes tasks that make others sit up and take notice. John Shaw Billings, the famous librarian, had this ability. To a friend who praised him for the performance of what others thought to be a most difficult task, he said:

"I'll let you into the secret—it is nothing really difficult if you only begin. Some people contemplate a task until it looks so big it seems impossible, but I just begin, and it gets done somehow. There would be no coral islands if the first bug sat down and began to wonder how the job was to be done."

II
PURPOSE FORMING

One of the interesting points the fascinated reader of biography comes to look for is the first hint of the formation of the purpose that later characterized the life of the subject. There is infinite variety, but in every case there is apt to be something that takes the purposeful reader back to the days when his own ambition was taking shape.

For instance, there is Daniel Boone. One would not be apt to select him as an example of one whose life was ruled by a purpose deliberately formed and adhered to for many years. Yet he had his vision of what he desired to accomplish when, at twenty-one years of age, he was marching from North Carolina to Pennsylvania to join Braddock's company. On the way he met John Finley, a hunter who had traveled through Ohio and into the wild regions to the south. His tale of Kentucky fired Boone's imagination, and the two men planned to go there just as soon as the trip to Fort Duquesne was at an end. It proved impossible to carry out the plan for many years, but Boone never lost sight of his purpose, and ultimately he carved out the Wilderness Road and opened the way for the pioneers to seek homes in the Kentucky Wilderness.

Alexander Hamilton was but twelve years old when he wrote from his home in St. Croix, in the West Indies, to a friend in America:

"I contemn the grovelling condition of a clerk, or the like, to which my fortune condemns me, and would willingly risk my life, though not my character, to exalt my station. I am confident, Ned, that my youth excludes me from any hope of immediate preferment, nor do I desire it, but I mean to prepare the way for futurity."

Not for a day did he lose sight of his purpose. The opportunity he sought came years later. He sailed for America, and began the career that led to usefulness and fame.

As a boy Robert Fulton was ambitious. He had two dreams. He wished to go to Europe to study art, and he wished to buy a farm for his widowed mother. For these objects he saved every dollar he could. On his twenty-first birthday he took his mother and sister to the home he had bought for them, and later in the same year he sailed for Europe.

When Peter Cooper was making his way against odds in New York City he felt the need of an education. But he had to work by day and there was no night school. Night after night he studied by the light of a tallow candle. And while he studied, his life purpose was formed: some day he would make it easy for apprentice boys to secure an education after working hours. Many years passed before he was able to carry this purpose into effect. By this time the apprentice system had been displaced, but he felt that young people still needed the school he had in mind. In 1859, nearly fifty years after his own boyhood struggle, he founded Cooper Union, in which thousands have had the opportunity "to open the volume of Nature by the light of truth—so unveiling the laws and methods of Deity that the young may see the beauties of creation, enjoy its blessings and learn to love the Being from whom cometh every good and perfect gift."

As a boy Abraham Lincoln made up his mind "to live like Washington." He was twenty-two years old when, in New Orleans,—where he had taken a flatboat loaded with produce—he saw a slave auction and spoke the never-to-be-forgotten words: "If ever I get a chance to hit that thing, I'll hit it hard." Thirty-five years later came his chance, and he did "hit that thing hard" with the Emancipation Proclamation.

Alexander Graham Bell's life ambition was to teach deaf children how to articulate. Funds were short. That he might have more funds he engaged in experiments that led to the invention of the telephone. When the telephone instrument was given the attention it deserved at the Philadelphia Centennial of 1876, the inventor wrote triumphantly to his parents: "Now I shall have the money to promote the teaching of speech to deaf children."

James Stewart, the Scotch boy who became a famous missionary in South Africa, was fifteen years old when, one day while following the plow in Perthshire, he began to brood over the future. "What was it to be?" The question flashed across his mind, "Might I not make more of my life than by remaining here?" Then he said, "God helping me, I will be a missionary." At another time, while hunting with a cousin, he said "Jim, I shall never be satisfied till I am in Africa with a Bible in my pocket and a rifle on my shoulder, to supply my wants."

James Robertson was a school teacher in Canada when he became a Christian. On the Sunday he was to take his vows as a follower of Christ, he walked two miles to church with a friend who has told of his memories of the day thus:

"As we went along the Governor's Road there was a bush, 'Light's Woods,' on the south side of the road. Robertson suggested that we turn aside into the bush, not saying for what purpose. We penetrated it a short distance, when, with a rising hill on our right and on comparatively level ground, the tall maples waving their lovely heads far above us, and the stillness of the calm, sunny day impressing us with a sense of the awful, we came to a large stone. Robertson proposed that we engage in prayer. We knelt down together. He prayed that he might be true to the vows he was about to take, true to God and ever faithful in his service."

From that day the young man's purpose was inflexible. He would be a minister. He did not dream of conspicuous places in the church. When the temptations came to seek place and position, he wrote to Miss Cowing, who had promised to be his wife, "We are no longer our own. The time for self is gone for us."

William Duncan likewise was tempted to seek a position of prominence. When he decided to become a missionary, his employers sought to dissuade him. "You have one of the keenest brains in England," one of them said. "Don't you see you are making a fool of yourself?" "Fool or no fool, my mind is made up, and nothing can change it," was the positive reply. And he set his face like a flint, and in time began the wonderful work that has written his name indelibly in the history of the Indians of Western Canada and Alaska.

Washington Gladden was a country newspaper man in Owego, New York, when he united with the church, and began to make definite plans for a larger future than he had yet dreamed of. First he went to the Academy and then to college, with the ministry always in view.

George Grenfell, who became a missionary in Africa, was thirteen years old when he began to think of devoting his life to work for others. The reading of Livingstone's first book turned his thoughts to Africa.

William Waddell was fifteen years old when he became a Christian. At the time he was working for a ship-joiner at Clydebank, Scotland. The ambition took possession of him to become a missionary to Africa. Neither lack of education nor scarcity of funds was allowed to stand in his way. He kept at his work until he saw an advertisement asking for men to go to the Orange Free State to assist in building a church. He volunteered, and, as a layman and a mechanic, began his wonderful career in Africa.

David Lloyd-George was an orphan in Wales when he determined to be a lawyer. So he read, under the guidance of his shoemaker uncle, and when he was fourteen he was ready for the preliminary examination. For six years more he continued his preparation. Before he was twenty-one he set out on the career that has made him the leader to whom King and people of England alike turned eagerly.

These men found their place and did their work, not because they sought great things for themselves, but because they lived in the spirit of the advice given by a celebrated Canadian to a company of young people:

"You cannot all attain high positions: there are not enough to go around. You cannot all be preachers or premiers, but you can all do thoroughly and well what is set you to do, and so fit yourselves for some higher duty, and thus by industry and fidelity and kindness you can fill your sphere in life and at last receive the 'Well done' of your Lord."

III
USING TIME WISELY

A remark made by an acquaintance in the street car showed such familiarity with the work and trials of the busy conductor that inquiry followed.

"Yes, I was a conductor once," the man said, "but I had my eye on something else. At night I took a business course, and soon was able to take a position with a railroad company."

"That was fine!" was the answering comment. "How you must have enjoyed resting on your oars as you reaped the fruits of extra toil."

"Enjoyment—yes! But rest—no!" came the reply. "I wasn't done. I still had my evenings, and I kept on studying. The things I learned in these extra hours came in handy when the Superintendent asked me to become his secretary."

Service in the railroad office was interrupted by enlistment in the army, although the worker was well beyond the age of the draft. "How could I think of anything but service at the front?" he said, with a matter-of-fact accent. While in the service the habit of study in spare hours persisted; becoming familiar with the military manual he attracted the attention of his officers, and was marked for added responsibility. At the close of the war he resumed his work for the railroad and entered a technical school which provides night courses for the ambitious.

Forty years of age, and still learning!

An employer has written of an employee who, ten years ago, was securing fifteen dollars per week. But he was studying, and he soon attracted the attention of the head of the business, who called him "a rough diamond." He knew that the ambitious man seemed to lack some of the vital elements of success. But he watched him as he took evening courses in business psychology and salesmanship. "This man is paid by me to-day from $12,500 to $15,000 a year," was the gratifying conclusion of the employer's story.

A great executive recently told in a magazine article of a young man in the office of his employment director who attracted attention because of an exceptionally pleasing personal appearance. Before the director saw him the executive asked him what he was studying. "When I left school," was the reply, made with something of a sneer, "I promised myself I would never open a book again as long as I lived, and I'm keeping my promise."

The executive was about to leave the office for a two weeks' vacation. First, however, he wrote a few words about the applicant, placed them in a sealed envelope, and left this with the employment director, to be kept for him. On his return he asked about the applicant, by name. The answer came, with prompt disgust:

"That fellow was the limit! Fired him two days after he was hired. Dead from the neck up!"

Then the sealed letter was produced and the message enclosed was read:

"You will hire A—— H—— on his looks. Within two weeks you will fire him. He's dead from his neck."

A writer in *Association Men* has made a comparison between two men, and the way they spent their leisure:

"Here is my friend Chris Hall—that is not his real name, but I assure you he is a real person. I like Chris, and so does everybody who knows him. He is honest and kind and clean, but in spite of these splendid characteristics he never makes progress. Five years ago he was promoted to his present position, and he draws as salary just about what he did then. And there is no prospect that he will ever draw much more. Yet he could make himself worth four times as much in a very short while—$200 a week instead of $50—if he would only fit himself for the job ahead. But he lives entirely in the present. Perhaps the best way to describe him is to give his diary for a week, a record of how he spent his time when not actually working. And, please notice that everything he did was perfectly legitimate and honorable; but also notice, that everything was for immediate personal pleasure:

Monday—Rainy evening; went to bed early after playing a while with the kids.
Tuesday—Strolled over to see Mollie's brother, who is just back from France; he looks well but would not talk much about the fighting; advised him not to hurry about getting a job, as he deserved a good long spell of rest after the hard campaign.
Wednesday—Left office early; first big league game this year; went around to the club and talked it all over with the boys after supper.
Thursday—Office closed all day on account of parade of returning troops; took Mollie and children to see it; awfully tired and went to bed early.

Friday—Sold my two Liberty Bonds which I had bought on installments; Mollie needed summer dresses and there were several small debts I had to pay; took Mollie to the movies after supper.

Saturday (afternoon)—Whole family went to Seaside Park by steamer—children enjoyed it for a while but soon got tired and fretful; what with the heat and the crowds and the late hour of getting home it really didn't pay.

Sunday—In bed till nearly noon; read the papers; changed the soil in Mollie's potted plants; afternoon, Tom and his wife and Charlie Nichols and his best girl came over and all stayed to supper; strolled over to Mother's and found everyone there.

"Over against that let me put a few lines from the diary of Elihu Burritt:

Monday—Headache; 40 lines Cuvier's 'Theory of the Earth'; 64 pages French; 11 hours forging.

Tuesday—60 lines Hebrew; 30 pages French; 10 pages Cuvier; 8 lines Syriac; 10 lines Danish; 10 lines Bohemian; 9 lines Polish; 15 names of stars; 10 hours forging.

Wednesday—25 lines Hebrew; 8 lines Syriac; 11 hours forging.

"Who was Elihu Burritt? He was a New England blacksmith who worked on an average 10 hours a day at his forge; but who studied in his spare moments until he became known and honored all over the world as 'the learned blacksmith.' He became great—not by forging—but by the way he used his afterwork hours."

IV
WORKING HARDER

"It was the rule of his life to study not how little he could do, but how much."

These words were spoken of a great publisher and might have been made the text of the volume issued to commemorate the centenary of the business house founded by the man of whom they were spoken.

The young man was sixteen when his father drove him from their country home to the city, and apprenticed him to a firm of printers.

As an apprentice he and another young man were frequently partners in working an old-fashioned hand press. "One applied the ink with hand-balls, and the other laid on sheets and did the pulling. They changed work at regular intervals, one inking and the other pulling." The biographer who gives this description of the work of the two, adds that his hero was accustomed to remain at his press after the other men had quit work whenever he could secure a partner to assist him.

The young man's fellow worker was often persuaded to assist him in these extra efforts—usually much against his will. While he often felt like rebelling because of his partner's ambition to do his utmost for his employers, he could not restrain his admiration for the man's industry.

Once the unwilling partner said: "Often, after a good day's work, he would say to me, 'Let's break the back of another token (two hundred and fifty impressions)—just break its back.' I would often consent reluctantly but he would beguile me, or laugh at my complaints, and never let me off till the token was completed, fair and square. It was a custom for us in the summer to do a clear half-day's work before the other boys and men got their breakfast. We would meet by appointment in the grey of the early morning and go down to the printing-room."

Fellow workmen made sport of the ambitious young man, not only because of what they felt was his excessive industry, but because of his homespun clothes and heavy cow-hide boots. He seldom retorted, but once, when jests had gone further than usual, he said to a tormentor: "When I am out of my time and set up for myself, and you need employment, as you probably will, come to me and I will give you work." The man little thought the prophecy would be fulfilled, but forty years after, when the industrious apprentice was mayor of the city and one of the world's leading publishers, he was reminded of the promise made to the tormentor, and the promised position was given to him. The workman who believed in doing more than was expected of him had won his way to fame and fortune, while his derider had made no progress.

In 1817 the industrious apprentice asked a brother—who in the meantime had served his apprenticeship in a printing office—to go into business with him. Later two other brothers were taken into the firm. All were believers in the doctrine that had led the oldest member of the firm to success—the doctrine of doing as much instead of as little as possible.

Their readiness to work constantly enabled the four brothers, who started with little capital except their knowledge of their trade, to build up within a generation one of the world's greatest publishing houses. They improved every moment. But they were never tempted to work on Sunday; business was never so pressing that they would break into the day of rest, or make their men do so. In this they were only living in accordance with purposes formed during their days of working for others. It is stated of one of the brothers, whose employer rejoiced in his readiness to do hard work and plenty of it, that he was expected to work on Sunday, in order to get ready the catalogue of an auction sale which was to be held next day. "That I will not do," he said, respectfully but firmly: "I cannot work on Sunday." He did work till midnight; then—in spite of the threat that he would be discharged—he laid down his composing stick on the case. On Monday morning his employer apologized and asked him to return to work.

Thirty-six years after the founding of the house, it occupied five five-story buildings on one street and six on another street. Then a careless plumber started a fire that—within a few hours—destroyed the entire property. But the energetic men who knew how to work were not discouraged at the thought of beginning again. The night after the fire they met for conference. As they separated one of them remarked that the evening had seemed more like a time of social festivity than a consultation over a great calamity.

Business associates hastened to make offers of loans. Within forty-eight hours the firm was tendered more than one hundred thousand dollars. Publishers offered their presses, printing material and office room. Authors wrote that they were ready to wait indefinitely for pay, while employees not only made a like suggestion, but said they were willing to have their pay reduced. While none of these offers were accepted, they were greatly appreciated, for they told of the place the brothers had won for themselves by untiring industry and sterling integrity.

After the fire the house became greater than ever, so that to-day it stands as an example of what "hard work coupled with high ideals" may accomplish. And to every young man the thought of it gives inspiration to follow in the steps of the founder who "made it the rule of his life to study not how little he could do, but how much."

V
ABUSING THE WILL TO WORK

There are times when the real test of a worker's courage is not his readiness to work but his will to curb the temptation to be intemperate in work.

When the word "intemperance" is mentioned most people think at once of strong drink; many people are unwilling to think of anything but strong drink. As if where there is no temptation to drink there can be no temptation to intemperance!

Paul had a different idea. When he wrote to the Corinthians, "Every man that striveth for the mastery is temperate in all things," he must have had in mind scores of different ways in which intemperance endangers success.

If people were to make a list of some of the aspects of intemperance that are characteristic of modern life, it is quite likely that a large proportion would omit one of the most serious of all—the intemperance of the man who lives to work, who drives himself to work, who is never happy unless he is working, who makes himself and others unhappy because he labors too long, and too persistently, perhaps with the result that his own promising career is wrecked and the industry of others is interfered with seriously.

One of the most striking illustrations of intemperance in work is supplied by the life of Samuel Bowles, editor of the Springfield, Massachusetts, *Republican,* one of the famous editors of the generation beginning a few years after the Civil War.

Mr. Bowles was but eighteen years old when he had his first warning that his system could not stand the strain of the work to which a strong will drove him. His mother used to set a rocking chair for him at the table at meal-time, because, as she said, "Sam has so little time to rest." But the rocking chair was empty for months, when a breakdown sent him South for a long period of recuperation.

When he returned home he plunged into work with all his might. "He worked late at night; vacations and holidays were unknown; of recreation and general society he had almost nothing," his biographer says. For years his office hours began before noon and continued until one or two in the morning. Finally the strain became too great, and loss of sight was feared. Still he forced himself to work, and the injury to his brain was begun that was later to cause his death. He would take a bottle of cold tea to the office, that by its use he might aid his will to work when nature said, "Stop!" For a long time his only sleep—and it was sadly broken sleep—was on a lounge in the office, from two to six or seven in the morning. Then he would set to work again. "By his unceasing mental activity he wore himself out," the comment was made on his career. "For the last twenty years of his life his nerves and stomach were in chronic rebellion. Heavy clouds of dyspepsia, sciatica, sleeplessness, exhaustion, came often and staid long."

The intemperate worker knew what he was doing. Once he wrote to a friend, "You can't burn the candle at both ends, and make anything by it in the long run; and it is the long pull that you are to rely on, and whereby you are to gain glory." Persistent headaches, "nature's sharp signal that the engine had been overdriven," added to the warning. At last, when he was thirty-seven, he wrote: "My will has carried me for years beyond my mental and physical power; that has been the offending rock. And now, beyond that desirable in keeping my temper, and forcing me up to proper exercise and cheerfulness through light occupation, I mean to call upon it not at all, if I can help it, and to do only what comes freely and spontaneously from the overflow of power and life. This will make me a light reader, a small worker."

Well for him if he had kept his resolution. Still he drove himself to work beyond what his body and brain could stand. Then came paralysis. "Nothing is the matter with me but thirty-five years of hard work," he said. At the time of his death he was not fifty-one years old.

His friends could not but admire him for strength of will, for achievement in the face of ill health, for triumph, by sheer will-power, over every obstacle except the will that drove him to his death. He accomplished much, but how much more he might have accomplished if he had been temperate in his use of the wonderful powers of mind and body which God had given him!

In connection with this glimpse of the life of one who illustrates the disaster brought by the will to be intemperate, it is helpful to think of the life of another American man of letters whose will to be temperate in his treatment of a body weak and frail prolonged life and usefulness.

Francis Parkman, the historian, was never a well man after his trip that resulted in the writing of *The Oregon Trail*. In fact, he was a physical wreck at twenty-five years of age. He could not even write his own name, until he first closed his eyes; he was unable to fix his mind on a subject, except for very brief intervals, and his nervous system was so exhausted that any effort was a burden. However, in spite of this limitation, which became worse, if possible, instead of better, he managed to accomplish an immense amount of the finest literary work by doing what he could and stopping when this was wise. His will to take care of himself was given the mastery of his will to work. For forty-four years after the completion of *The Oregon Trail* he labored on, preparing history after history. He was seventy years old when he died, leaving behind him achievements that would have been a tremendous task for a man in perfect health.

To everyone is given the marvelous equipment of body and brain, as well as the will which makes possible their judicious investment or their prodigal waste in the struggle to make life count.

CHAPTER FOUR

THE COURAGE OF FACING CONSEQUENCES

Y OUNG people sometimes play the game of "Consequences." The sport increases in proportion to the strangeness of the results.

Perhaps the reason the game has so many attractions is the fact that life is a long story of consequences.

There are people who do not like to play the game of life seriously because they say the consequences of self-denial and self-sacrifice are too uncertain; they prefer the cowardice of inaction to the courage of purposeful living.

The folks worth while are those who, refusing to be troubled by what may or may not be the consequences of their acts, still have the pluck to go on with what they know is right. Let the results be what they may, they propose to be straightforward and true. This is the courage that counts.

There may be uncertainty as to the specific form the results of their stand may take, yet that result is sure to be pleasing and helpful.

I
VENTURING

When Washington Irving was about to return to America from Madrid, where he had been minister of the United States to the court of Spain, the Philadelphia house that had been publishing his books, discouraged by the decreasing sales, sent word to him that the public was not able to appreciate his books, and they would have to allow them to go out of print. The books had been printed directly from the type, so there were no plates which another publisher might use to bring out further editions at small expense.

The author, who was then sixty-five years of age, sorrowfully accepted the verdict of his publisher, and planned to take desk-room in the New York office of his brother, John Treat Irving, where he hoped to make a living by the practice of law.

But this was not to be. In New York was a young publisher who believed that Washington Irving's works were classics, and that the American public would buy them eagerly if properly approached. Friends told him that he might make a mistake, but he had the courage to go ahead. So he wrote to the discouraged author what must have seemed to other publishers a daring letter; he proposed to publish new editions of all Irving's old books, on condition that new books, also, be given to him; and he promised that royalties for the first year should be at least one thousand dollars, for the second year two thousand dollars, and for the third year three thousand dollars.

When Irving received the letter, he kicked over the desk in front of him, at the same time saying to his brother:

"There is no necessity, John, for my bothering with the law. Here is a fool of a publisher going to give me a thousand dollars a year for doing nothing."

But the publisher was not so foolish as he seemed. His promises were more than made good. Sales were large. Other authors were attracted, until the publishing house became one of the leaders among American publishers.

Nine years later Washington Irving had an opportunity to show his gratitude. Just before the panic of 1857 a young man whom the generous publisher had taken into partnership, involved him seriously. The defalcations were not discovered until the accidental death of the partner. Thus weakened, the firm was unable to survive the panic; its affairs were put in the hands of a receiver, and all accounts were sold. At the age of forty-two, the head of the firm bravely faced the necessity of beginning life over.

At the receiver's sale Washington Irving bought the plates of all his books. A number of publishers offered him fancy terms if he would permit them to bring out new editions, but he turned a deaf ear to their entreaties and offered the plates to their former owner, to be paid for in annual installments. Touched by the gratitude of his friend, the publisher accepted the offer.

The author never had cause to regret his action. During the years that elapsed before his death the results of the new venture were more satisfactory than ever. The courageous action of both publisher and author had been amply vindicated by results.

II
FORMING CHARACTER

The best time to learn the courage that proves so effective in the struggle of life is in youth. More than fifty years ago two boys in Scotland were hunting rabbits. Tiring of the comparatively easy hunting on the ground, they looked longingly at a cliff of hard clay several hundred feet high, in whose precipitous side were many rabbit burrows. They managed to climb the cliff. At length they were making their way along an almost perpendicular parapet, cutting their way with their knives. Then one of the boys fell, with a scream, to the bottom of the cliff. There was a moment of terror. This was succeeded by a grim determination to go forward, the only way of escape. Driving his knife deep in the clay, he rested on this for a moment. That moment, it has always since seemed to him, marked the first momentous period in his life, the time when his personality first emerged into consciousness. He says: "I whispered to myself one word, 'Courage!' Then I went on with my work." At length he reached the ground.

The lesson learned at such fearful cost told emphatically on the boy's character. From that day he showed that there was in him the making of a man who would not be balked by unfavorable circumstances. He did not understand how or why, but he felt that new will-power had come to him with the appeal to himself to take courage in the face of death.

A few years later he went to Brazil. A Spaniard told him that moral deterioration within six months was all but certain to come to every young man who began life there. But he was determined not to give way to bad habits. When he reached Santos, his companions urged him to give himself up to all kinds of vice; they told him that it was either this or death, or perhaps something worse than death. They emphasized their words by pointing to a young man who had determined to keep straight, and had been left to himself until he was demented. But the boy who had learned courage on the precipice made up his mind that he must live as God wished him to live, and he turned a deaf ear to all entreaties.

Another book of biography tells of a boy who delighted in playing cards with his father and mother. But when he united with the Church and became President of the Christian Endeavor Society he began to wonder if he was doing right. One night his father took up the cards and called him to play whist.

"I don't think I'll play whist any more," he said quietly. "I've been thinking that perhaps it wasn't right for me to play."

"Are you setting yourself up to judge your father and mother, young man?" his father asked, sternly.

"No, I didn't say it isn't all right for you to play," was the reply. "But you know I am President of the Christian Endeavor Society and some of the members don't think it is right to play. So I guess I'd better not."

His father looked at him thoughtfully for a minute, then picked up the cards and threw them back into the drawer.

"Charlie," he said, "I want you to understand that I think you have done a manly thing to-night, and I honor you for your courage."

That was the end of whist in that house.

Courage showed itself in much the same way in the life of J. Marion Sims, the great surgeon. He used to tell how, when he was a boy at a South Carolina School, he was able to take a stand that had its effect on his whole after-life. Many of his fellow students were sons of wealthy planters, and their habits were not always the best. On several occasions they tried to lead him into mischief. They were particularly anxious to make him a companion in their drinking bouts. Twice he gave way to their pleas, but after sorrowful experience of the results of his lapses, he decided to make a brave stand. So he said to his tempters:

"See here, boys, you can all drink, and I cannot. You like wine and I do not. I hate it; its taste is disagreeable, its effects are dreadful, because it makes me drunk. Now, I hope you all will understand my position. I don't think it is right for you to ask me to drink wine when I don't want it, and when it produces such a bad effect on me."

To say this required real courage, but the results were good, not only in himself, but also, fortunately, in some of his companions.

III
TRUTH TELLING

Those who, in early life, learn to be courageous in the face of difficult tasks will be ready for the temptation that is apt to come to most young people to compromise with what they know to be right and true, to allow an exception "just this once!" in the straightforward course they have marked out for themselves. And the worst of it is that such a temptation is apt to come without the slightest warning and to present itself in such a light that it is easy to find an excuse for yielding, and to deem it quixotic and unreasonable not to yield.

Once a young teacher who later became famous at Harvard, had occasion to censure a student who had given, as he believed, the wrong solution of a problem. On thinking the matter over at home, he found that the pupil was right and the teacher wrong. It was late at night and in the depth of winter, but he immediately started for the young man's room, at some distance from his own home, and asked for the man he had wronged. The delinquent, answering with some trepidation the untimely summons, found himself the recipient of a frank apology.

"Why, in the name of reason, do you walk a mile in the rain for a perfectly unimportant thing?" this man was asked on another occasion. "Simply because I have discovered that it was a misstatement, and I could not sleep comfortably till I put it right," was the reply.

Again the story is told of him that he borrowed a friend's horse to ride to a town where he expected to take the stage. He promised to leave the animal at a certain stable in the town. Upon reaching the place he found that the stage was several miles upon its way. This was a serious disappointment. A friend urged him to ride to the next town, where he could come up with the vehicle, promising himself to send after the borrowed horse and forward it to its owner. The temptation to accept the offer was great. The roads were ankle deep in mud, and the stage rapidly rolling on its way. The only obstacle was his promise to leave the horse at the appointed place. He declined the friendly offer, delivered the horse as he had promised, and, shouldering his baggage, set off on foot through the mud to catch the stage.

At this time he was eighteen years old, but he had learned the lesson that made him remarkably efficient and dependable through life.

Dr. W. T. Grenfell has told of a hardy trapper in Labrador, the partner of a man who was easily discouraged; the arrangement was that they should share equally the hardships and the rewards of the trapping expeditions. Both were very poor. The stronger man was most unselfish in his treatment of his associate. One winter their lives were all but lost during the severity of a storm which burst on them while they were setting their traps on an ice-girt island. On reaching the mainland the timid man insisted on dissolving the partnership; he was unwilling to repeat the risks, even for the sake of his needy family. In a few days the hardy trapper revisited the traps on the mainland. To his great joy he found in one trap a magnificent silver fox, whose skin was worth five hundred dollars—a fortune to the Labrador trapper, especially welcome during that hard winter. "How glad I am the partnership has been dissolved, and that the fox is all mine," was his first thought. But first thought was not allowed to be last thought. There was a struggle. At length the decision was made that the needy man who had set the trap with him should share in the prize; the argument that he had forfeited all right to a share was not allowed to weigh against the unselfish arguments for division.

A friend of young people has told of an incident which occurred in a great Boston department store where she sought to match some dress goods. After turning away from several discourteous clerks she showed her sample to a salesman who gave respectful attention to her. Glancing at the slits cut in the side of the bit of goods, he remarked:

"That isn't one of my samples. I will ask the clerk who mailed this sample to wait on you."

"But I don't want any other clerk to wait on me," responded the women, hastily, fearing that the sample might have come originally from one of the discourteous clerks first encountered; "I want you to have this sale."

"If you had asked for goods of that quality, width and price, without showing me the sample, I could have found it for you at once," replied the clerk, with a smile, "but now, this sale belongs to the clerk who sent out the sample."

"Then I won't give you this sample to hunt it up by," said the woman, wishing to see if she could carry her point, and she proceeded to tuck the sample away in her purse.

"But I know that I have seen it, and my conscience knows it," was the clerk's comment, as he laughingly laid his hand on his heart and turned to look for the other salesman.

The purchaser went on to tell thus of the salesman's unerring loyalty to his principles: "In a moment he returned. The other clerk was at lunch. What a sigh of relief I gave! 'I will make out the sale and turn it over to him when he comes in,' he said, displaying the shining black folds of the goods I desired."

A real estate dealer in a Texas city was once tempted to be false to his principles, "just once," when he felt sure a sale depended on it. His prospective customer was a foreigner, who wished the salesman to drink with him after a trip to examine the property on Saturday and then to promise to make an engagement to continue the search next morning. But the business man was opposed to the use of liquor, and he had never done business on Sunday. What was he to do on this occasion? Would it hurt anything if he should make an exception in favor of this customer who could not be expected to understand his scruples?

The temptation was acute; but it was conquered. Respectfully but firmly the buyer was told why the salesman could not join him in taking a drink, and why he could not go with him again until Monday morning. The man went away in a rage.

Next morning the real estate man saw the foreigner in the hands of a rival. "That sale is gone!" he thought. When three days more passed without the return of the buyer he decided that he had paid heavily for being true to his better self.

But on Thursday evening the foreigner sought the conscientious real estate dealer and surprised him by saying:

"Those other fellows showed me lots of farms, but you wouldn't drink with me, nor show me land on Sunday because you think it wrong. So, maybe, I think you won't lie to me. I buy my farm of you."

Many times the reward of being true to one's conscience will not come so promptly—except in the satisfaction the man has in knowing that he has done the right thing. But the sure result is to bring him a little nearer to the great reward that must come to a man whose integrity has stood the test of years—the appreciation of those who know him and their confidence in his honor.

IV
DUTY DOING

It is not always necessary that a man should be aquainted with another to be able to repose implicit confidence in him. A life of fearless, straightforward duty-doing will inevitably leave its record in the face. Sometimes a frank, open countenance that cannot be misread is far better than any letter of introduction.

"We are suspicious of strangers," a man said to one who had sought at his hands a favor that called for trust; then he added, with a smile, "but some faces are above suspicion," and proceeded, with overwhelming generosity, to grant far more than had been asked.

Years ago a business man unexpectedly found himself without sufficient funds to continue his journey through Europe. As this was before the days of travelers' checks or the ocean cable, he was at a loss what to do. In his uncertainty he went to an Italian banking house and asked them to cash a large draft on his home bank. After an instant's pause the request was granted. Years later the merchant again saw the accommodating banker, and asked why a stranger was given such a large sum. "In plain truth, it was just your honest face, and nothing else," was the reply. On another trip abroad the merchant had a similar experience. During a thunderstorm he took refuge with his wife in a curio shop. The English-speaking woman in charge was so cordial, and her goods were so pleasing, that the visitor said he would have liked to make some purchase, but his remaining funds were not more than sufficient for his journey home. The reply was: "Take whatever you please, sir. No one could look in your face and distrust you."

A similar story was told by a Russian Jew who entered New York a penniless immigrant. After a disheartening period of working in the sweatshop he saw an opportunity to start in business for himself. But he had no capital. At a venture he asked a business man to trust him for the stock in trade. After gazing at him closely the man said, "You have a credit face, so I will do as you ask."

It is worth while to have a face that insures confidence. But let it be remembered that the possession of such a face is not an accident; it belongs only to those who have the courage to think honestly, deal fairly and live truly.

V
FINDING HIS LIFE

During the boyhood of Charles Abraham Hart, who was later the youngest soldier in the War with Spain, he was on confidential terms with his mother. One day when they were visiting together, she asked him about something that had happened the winter before, which she was unable to understand. His father had given to him and to his brothers two dollars each to spend for Christmas presents. William spent the entire sum, but Charles bought cheap presents, and it was evident that he had kept back a part of the amount. Other members of the family misunderstood him, but his mother thought she knew him well enough to be sure he had done nothing selfish.

The record of the conversation between mother and son is told in the boy's biography:

"The presents you bought were very cheap presents," she said to him. "I don't think they could have cost more than seventy-five cents."

"They cost sixty-five cents," he told her.

"And your father asked what you had done with the rest of your money, and you said you didn't want to tell him."

"Yes, I remember that father thought I was stingy, too."

"Do you mind telling me now what you did with the money?"

The boy did not answer for a few moments. Then he said, quietly:

"I bought a Bible for Fred Phillips. He didn't have a good Bible, and I thought he needed one more than you and the boys needed expensive presents."

"But why didn't you tell your father?"

"Because Fred was ashamed not to be able to buy the Bible for himself, and he wouldn't take mine until I had promised that I wouldn't tell anybody that I had given it to him. Since Fred has moved to Boston, I feel he wouldn't care if I told you. I want you to know, for I just heard to-day that Fred has joined the church. Isn't that good news?"

"Yes, indeed. Perhaps your giving him the Bible helped him to do it, too. Charles, when you get to be a man, do you suppose you will always be so careless of how others may misunderstand you?"

"I am not careless of that now," he declared. "The desire to be popular is one of the things I have to fight against all the time."

What shall we choose? Comfort of service? Ease, or honorable performance of duty? The desire for popularity, or the purpose to be of use? Service is the best way to find comfort; honorable performance of duty is the sure road to the only ease worth while, and thoughtfulness for others is the open sesame to popularity.

There is nothing new in this statement. It is only one of the thousand and one possible applications of the lesson taught by the great Teacher when He said, "He that loseth his life for My sake shall find it."

CHAPTER FIVE

COURAGE FOR THE SAKE OF OTHERS

FROM Norway comes a moving tale of a lighthouse keeper. One day he went to the distant shore for provisions. A storm arose, and he was unable to return. The time for lighting the lamp came, and Mary, the elder child, said to her little brother, "We must light the lamp, Willie." "How can we?" was his question. But the two children climbed the long narrow stairs to the tower where the lamp was kept. Mary pulled up a chair and tried to reach the lamp in the great reflector; it was too high. Groping down the stairs she ascended again with a small oil lamp in her hand. "I can hold this up," she said. She climbed on the chair again, but still the reflector was just beyond her reach. "Get down," said Willie, "I know what we can do." She jumped down and he stretched his little body across the chair. "Stand on me," he said. And she stood on the little fellow as he lay across the chair. She raised the lamp high, and its light shone far out across the water. Holding it first with one hand, then with the other, to rest her little arms, she called down to her brother, "Does it hurt you, Willie?" "Of course it hurts," he called back, "but keep the light burning."

The boy was wise beyond his years. He would do the important thing, no matter how it hurt. Here the thing of chief importance was looking out for the men at sea. To put them first took real courage. But what of it? That is the attitude toward life of the worker worth while; he does not stop to ask, "Is this easy?" Instead he asks, "Is this necessary? Will it be helpful?" Having answered the question he proceeds to do his best. It may hurt at first, but the time will come when it will hurt so much to leave the service undone that the inconvenience involved in doing it is lost sight of.

I
IMPARTING COURAGE

A young man won local fame as a bicycle long-distance rider. But over-fatigue, possibly coupled with neglect, caused contraction of certain muscles. He was unable to stand erect. He walked with bent back, like an old man. "What useful work can he do, handicapped as he is?" his friends asked.

But he did not lose courage. He continued to smile and make cheer for others. Finally he secured work in the office of the supervisor of a National Forest. And he made good. Most of his activities were at the desk; when he sat there his back was normal.

According to the idea of many, it would have been enough for the crippled man to look out for himself. What could he do for others? But he had not been trained in such a school; the cheerfulness that enabled him to be useful made it impossible for him to see another in need and not plan to do something for him.

The man who needed him was at hand—a cripple, whose feet were clumsy, misshapen. No one else thought that anything could be done for him but to speak dolefully and to assure him that he was fortunate in having parents and brothers who would look out for him.

But the man in the Forestry Service urged the cripple to apply for a summer appointment on the rocky, windy summit of a mountain nine thousand feet high. There it would be his duty to keep a vigilant eye on the forest stretching far away below his lofty eyrie, and to report the start of a forest fire. At first he laughed at the idea; had he not been told that he could never hope to do anything useful? Yet as he listened to his friend his eyes began to sparkle. Finally he dared to agree to make application for the position.

During the winter months the forester spent many evenings with his friend, coaching him in some of the lore of the forests, giving him books to read, and showing him what his specific duties would be, and how to perform them.

In the spring the situation was secured, and when the season of forest fires came the young man bravely climbed the steep trail over the snow to his lonely cabin. An able-bodied man is able to make the climb from the end of the wagon road in much less than an hour; the cripple required more than five hours to reach the top. Then he took up his residence there, cooking his own food, making his observations from morning until night, receiving his mother and his brothers when from time to time they came to see how he was getting on and to help him in some of the rougher tasks about the cabin. They thought they would need to speak words of cheer to a lonely, discouraged man, but they soon learned their error; not only did he have cheer enough for himself, but he was able to send his visitors away happier than when they came because of their contact with the man for whom life had been made over by the acts of a thoughtful friend, a friend whose own courage had been increased by his efforts to encourage a friend.

II
CONQUERING HAPPINESS

In a volume of short stories published some years ago there is included the vivid narrative of two humble citizens of an Irish village, a husband and wife, upon whom hard times have come. The husband is too feeble to make his living as of old at his trade as a road-mender. Their only hope is a son in America, and not a word comes from him, so they are compelled to go to the poor house.

Friends condole with them, and they are sad enough to suit the notions of those who feel that an awful ending is coming to their lives. One of the saddest of their friends is their physician who dreads going to see the unhappy old people in their new home. At last, however, he drives to the entrance to the poor farm. There he has his first surprise. Instead of seeing the disreputable place he had been accustomed to, he notices that the gate is on its hinges, the weeds by the side of the driveway are no longer in evidence, and an attempt has been made to give the house itself a more presentable appearance. About the doors are no discontented-looking old people, quarreling with one another. And when the wife of the poor farm keeper answers his knock at the door, the doctor hardly recognizes her; instead of a discouraged-looking slattern she is actually neat and cheerful looking.

"You wonder what has happened here, don't you?" the woman remarks. "It's all because of those blessed old folks you are asking for. They were disheartened, just at first, but soon they began to do helpful things for the rest of the folks. That cheered us all up, and it's made a different place of the farm."

The doctor's errand that day is to take word to the couple that their son from America wishes them to spend the remainder of their days with him. He has expected them to be overjoyed by the news. But, after talking together of the invitation, they assure him that their place is where they are. "We be road-mending here, making ways smoother for the folks that have rough traveling," is the explanation. "We think we ought to bide at the farm."

Thus the old people took the way of conquering unhappiness made known so long ago by Him who set the example of finding joy in caring for other people, the way taken by a modern follower of His who wrote home from the army:

"I cast my lot where I knew the road would be rough, and why should I complain? It seems to me at times that I must give way to my lower self and let the work slip off my back on others perhaps more tired than myself. But I have a tender, kind Father in heaven who tells me that my way is right. I have very little to uphold me in this work away from my friends. My happy moments are those which I spend with my Bible during my night watches, or thinking of happy days gone by, or building me air-castles for days to come. I am happy, too, when I read the little verse written in the front of my Testament, and so thankful for the power to understand it:

> "So nigh is grandeur to our dust,
>   So near is God to man,
> When duty whispers low, 'Thou must,'
>   The youth replies, 'I can.'"

Yet there are those who insist that it is the duty of one whose lot is hard to be morose and sad; that by covering his sadness with the gladness of service he is making a cheat of himself! In verse a writer with insight has pilloried such critics:

"He went so blithely on his way,
  The way men call the way of life,
  That good folks who had stopped to pray,
  Shaking their heads, were wont to say,
  It was not right to be so gay
  Upon that weary road of strife.

"He whistled as he went, and still
  He bore the young where streams were deep,
  He helped the feeble up the hill,
  He seemed to go with heart athrill,
  Careless of deed and wild of will—
  He whistled, that he might not weep."

III
MAKING LITTLE THINGS COUNT

There are people who spend so much time looking for the large, spectacular opportunities for serving others, that they pass by as unworthy of notice the opportunities for doing what seem to be little kindnesses. Fortunately, however, there are people who are so taken up with rendering what they call little services, that they have no time to worry because the big opportunities do not come their way.

A magazine writer tells of one of these doers of simple kindnesses:

"I was the shabbiest girl in the office," she says. "It was no one's fault and no one's shame that we were poor. I had intelligence enough to know that. I knew, too, what a sacrifice mother had made to pay for my tuition at business school. Still, the knowledge of my shabby clothes forced itself upon me, particularly my old black skirt! Mother had cleaned it and pressed it and cleaned it, but it seemed bent with age, and all the office girls looked so fresh and pretty in their trim business suits. I imagined all the first morning that they were pitying me and felt them looking at my shabbiness, and during noon hour I was so miserable; but when I went back next morning, I noticed that one of the girls had on nearly as old clothes as I did, and she was so nice to me that I fancied she was glad I had come because of our mutual poverty. Not until after I earned enough money to buy some suitable, nice clothes did I realize that the 'poor girl,' as I thought her, had drifted back into the prettiest, most tasteful clothes worn by any of the girls. She had only borne me company at a most trying time, and she knew, because her fellow-workers all admired her, that the little object lesson would keep them from hurting my feelings. The day has come now when new clothes are usual, when I may even achieve an appearance that is known as 'stylish.' But in my office, when a girl comes in shabby, painfully sensitive, as I was, I 'bear her company' until the better times shall come."

From another observer comes the story of the simple deeds of kindness done by a company of young people in Brooklyn to a young woman married to an elderly and uncongenial man. She showed symptoms of taking her life into her own hands. She felt that the world owed her happiness, and she was tempted to take it anywhere it might be found, especially in one undesirable direction. She was poor and outside of many ordinary social pleasures. The word was passed along the line that Mrs. D... needed especial attention and friendliness shown her. Immediately one girl, whose notice was in itself a compliment, invited her to attend a concert with her. Two more volunteered to see her home from Sunday school, and call for her as well. Books were loaned her, calls made, and in brief, a rope of warm sturdy hands steadying her over the hard place in the road, until she found herself and settled down to the duty she was on the point of leaving forever.

The widespread hunger for such little kindnesses was shown one day when a New York man accosted in Central Park a poor foreigner, who could speak little English. Noting that the man looked dejected, he offered him his hand. Then he asked the man if he was in need. "No, I don't need money," was the reply; "I was just hungry for a handshake." Blessings on those who are not too busy to think of the poor who are hungry for the little services they can render.

If they could know the ultimate effect of some of their deeds, these would not always seem insignificant. The man who is always on the lookout for little chances for service is more apt to perform services that are of great importance, than the man who spends his time dreaming of big things he will do some day.

IV
DID HE GO TOO FAR?

When an urgent call went out from Washington for physicians to go to France for hospital work among the men of the American Expeditionary Force, a specialist in a city of the Middle West decided to respond. Of course some of his friends told him he was foolish; they urged that he was needed for service at home. "Let doctors go who can be spared better than you," they said. "Think of the great work you are doing—work that will be more than ever necessary because thousands of others are leaving practices and going to the Front. Think of your past—how you worked your way through medical college at cost of severe toil; think of your family and the increasing demands on you; think of the future—what will become of your lucrative practice?"

The specialist did think of these things; he had delayed decision because the arguments had presented themselves forcibly to his own mind.

At last, however, his mind was made up. He would go to France. He would leave his patients in charge of two capable friends who would do everything possible to turn over, on the return of the volunteer, the lucrative office practice built up through many years.

He spent six months in camp with the members of the hospital unit of which he was given charge. Just before he went "over there" a friend said to him:

"It is fortunate that your practice is to be cared for so efficiently."

"What's that?" was the reply. "Oh, you mean the colleagues who took over my patients? They, too, have enlisted, and will soon be going abroad."

"But what of your $35,000 income?" was the dismayed rejoinder. "Surely you haven't the courage to give up all that!"

The major snapped his fingers, and said, with a smile, "*That* for the practice! It is my business to respond to my country's call. Don't talk of the sacrifice. What if I do have to start all over again when I come home? Just now I don't have to think about that."

This incident came to mind when reading in a popular weekly a telling story, camouflaged as to names, location and business, but recorded as the experience of a captain of industry. The story made him a manufacturer of shoes who, in the beginning, was rejoicing that his plants were running full time, turning out so many shoes for the regular trade that the profits of the year were bound to be tremendous. With others, he heard the plea of the Government for shoes for the soldiers. Carefully he assured himself that he would not need to respond; there were many manufacturers who would rush headlong for government contracts. When he learned that there were not enough volunteers he felt uncomfortable. Then, to his relief, he was asked to take the chairmanship of the subcommittee on shoes of the State Council of Defense.

"I'll do it!" he decided. "That will let me out honorably. As chairman I shall be criticized if I bid on the contracts myself."

Of course he learned his mistake. At length he decided to turn over one of his six plants to government contracts. The decision made him feel quite virtuous. Content was his only a little while, however. So he decided to devote another plant. Yet when he made his figures he thought he would add five cents a pair to his bid, as an extra margin of safety. Again his calculations were upset when his son told him that he had enlisted.

"That wasn't necessary," the father said. "What made you do it?"

"Why, dad, you know you'd expect me to feel ashamed if you didn't do just every little thing you could in a business way to help win this war—if you held back a shoe that would help the Government or charged a cent more than you ought to. You furnish the shoes and I'll furnish the shoots!"

Of course more had to be done after that. Soon half the plants were enlisted for the country. Surely nothing more could be asked than that he should go fifty-fifty, half for the country and half for himself.

The remainder of the story can be imagined—in one form it was lived out in the experience of millions. "Why don't you have done with that half-way patriotism?" came a voice that he could not silence.

The battle between Patriotism and Private Profits was decided gloriously —in the only possible manner. Away with fifty per cent. patriotism! Every one of the plants was put on Government orders.

Naturally there were those who asked, "Was such a sacrifice necessary?" But the reply was convincing.

That is the question that has been asked of Christians ever since the day when Christ said to Peter and Andrew, "Follow me." Our hearts are stirred by the simple record of what followed: "Straightway they left their nets,"—their livelihood, their associates, their families, their position in the world, everything—"and followed Him." The question was put to Prince Gallitzin when he renounced title and fortune and went to the mountains of Pennsylvania to make a home for some of his oppressed Russian countrymen. The words were hurled at the son of a wealthy English brewer, because he decided that if he would obey Christ fully he must renounce the source of his wealth as well as the money that had been made in an unrighteous business. The inquiry was heard many times by Matthias W. Baldwin, the builder of Old Ironsides and founder of the Baldwin Locomotive Works, when he gave up the making of jewelry because he thought that, as a Christian man, he ought to make his talents count for something more worth-while, and later on when he insisted on borrowing from the banks in time of financial panic to pay his pledges to Christian work.

Still the query persists, as it will persist long as the world stands.

You have heard it yourself, if you, like Caleb of old, are trying to follow God wholly. "Was the sacrifice necessary?"

Beware of the question, for it is a temptation to slack service, though often spoken by one who would show himself a friend. Necessary? Of course. Isn't it involved in courageous following of Christ?

CHAPTER SIX

GOLDEN RULE COURAGE

> "There is so much good in the worst of us,
> And so much bad in the best of us,
> That it hardly becomes any of us
> To talk about the rest of us."

THAT popular rhyme hits the nail squarely on the head. We are not to judge others. The world would be a pleasanter dwelling place if we would lay aside our critical attitude, and look on the best side of the men and women about us. Instead, however, it sometimes seems as if we were determined to forget all the good, and remember only the evil. Our additions to the comments of others are not praise, but blame. We do not seek to correct an unfavorable comment by saying, "But think of the good there is in his life"; we insist on drowning merited praise by saying, "But think how selfish he is; how careless of the comfort of others!" That is the cowardly thing to do. And life calls for courage.

The worst thing about the maker of such comments is that the readier he is to see—or imagine—faults in another, the more blind he is apt to become to faults in himself. This inability to see his own shortcomings would be ludicrous if it were not so pitiful. Yet these shortcomings are apparent to all who know him. Jesus, who knew human nature, said, "Judge not, that ye be not judged . . . first cast out the beam out of thine own eye; then shalt thou see clearly to cast out the mote out of thy brother's eye."

The courageous task of reforming ourselves seems prodigious when we think what good opinions we have of ourselves and what poor opinions we have of others, but the task is not impossible, for God has promised to give us the help we need, and He will never disappoint us. An earthly father knows how to give good things to his children; shall not the Heavenly Father do as much and more?

Since we have such a Father, it is the least we can do to learn of Him the true philosophy of life. Listen while He tells us what it is:

"All things, therefore, whatsoever ye would that men should do unto you, even so do ye also unto them."

Impossible and impracticable? Let us see.

I
LOOKING OUT FOR OTHERS

The president of a big manufacturing concern, who is also its active operating head, is quoted as saying that he finds a growing tendency among young men to go after business by sharp practice when they cannot get it any other way. They will "cut the corners of a square deal to land an order." In applying for positions, he goes on to say, some young fellows have tried to recommend themselves by telling how they got orders for former employers by some neat trick.

"I have had to tell them, square and plain," he adds, "that there wasn't any recommendation in that kind of talk with me. I have made up my mind that I am going to write out some plain talks on righteousness and post them up around the offices and shops where everybody will have a chance to read them. I have explained my plan about these bulletins to a number of other manufacturers, and I think several of them are going to do the same thing. Besides the moral reasons for the policy, it's the only policy to build up a sound business on. Take even the men who would be willing to make profit for themselves by shady deals, and they all want to buy goods for themselves of a firm that they can depend on. I think our history this past year has proved the wisdom of it; business has been rolling in from points that we never had an idea of getting anything from. The Golden Rule works."

Nathan Strauss was once asked what contributed most to his remarkable success. "I always looked out for the man at the other end of the bargain," he said.

In 1901 the State of Wisconsin struck a beautiful bronze medal in honor of Professor Stephen Moulton Babcock, the inventor of the milk test machine. Professor Babcock, so one admirer says, "knew its value to farmer and dairyman. He also knew its possibilities of fortune for himself. This invention has 'increased the wealth of nations by many millions of dollars and made continual new developments possible in butter and cheesemaking.' All this Professor Babcock knew it would do when he announced his discovery in a little bulletin to the farmers of Wisconsin. But at the bottom of that bulletin he added the brief and unselfish sentence, 'this test is not patented.' With that sentence he cheerfully let a fortune go. He wanted his invention to help other people, rather than make himself rich."

What a difference it would make if everyone should take the Golden Rule as the motto for each day, asking Christ's help in living in accordance with it! What a difference it would make in every home if father and mother and all the sons and daughters should resolve to make theirs a Golden-Rule household! The first thing necessary in bringing about such a change in the home is for one member to make the resolution and to do his best to live up to it. Others will follow inevitably when they note his careful, unselfish life and helpful acts.

There is a Jewish tradition that a Gentile came to Hillel asking to be taught the law, in a few words, while he stood on one foot. The answer was given, "Whatsoever thou wouldst that men should not do to thee, that do not thou to them." This was good, as far as it went, but there was nothing positive about it. Christ's teaching supplies the lack, showing what we are to do as well as what we are to leave undone. Christ always gives the touch required to make old teachings glow with life.

II
SUCCEEDING BY COURAGEOUS SERVICE

When John E. Clough was a student working his way through college, he was employed in a menial capacity at a hotel in a western town. His employer was absent for a season and the student was compelled to take charge of the hotel. He was successful, for he learned how to handle men of many sorts, how to provide for their comfort, how to make them feel that he was doing his best for them.

Years later, when he was a missionary in India, it became necessary for him to plan for the temporary entertainment of the men and women who came to the mission station by hundreds, and even by thousands, seeking Christian baptism. For days it was necessary to provide for their comfort. Many men would have been dismayed by the task, but to Dr. Clough the problem presented was simple; he had only to do on a large scale the very things which made his boyhood efforts at hotel-keeping such a pronounced success.

Experience in a hotel is a good course of preparation for any young man, whether he plans to be a missionary or to serve in any of the home callings that demand the Christian's time and thought. However, it is not possible for more than a very small proportion of young people to serve a period in a hotel; so it will be helpful to them to read some of the suggestions that have been made by a successful hotel proprietor. Those who heed these suggestions are apt to be successful in dealing with men and women anywhere.

It is worth while to note some of these rules:

"The hotel is operated primarily for the benefit and convenience of its guests.

"Any member of our force who lacks the intelligence to interpret the feeling of good will that this hotel holds toward its guests, cannot stay here very long.

"Snap judgments of men often are faulty. The unpretentious man with the soft voice may possess the wealth of Croesus.

"You cannot afford to be superior or sullen with any patron of the hotel.

"At rare intervals some perverse member of our force disagrees with a guest as to the rightness of this or that. . . . Either may be right. . . . In all discussions between hotel employees and guests, the employee is dead wrong from the guest's standpoint, and from ours. . . .

"Each member of our force is valuable only in proportion to his ability to serve our guests.

"Every item of extra courtesy contributes towards a better pleased guest, and every pleased guest contributes toward a better, bigger hotel...."

Yet a young man should not have to go to a hotel to learn these lessons. They were taught in the Book that every one of us should know better than any other book in our library. Listen to these messages of the Book, and compare them with the rules of the hotel:

"Not looking each of you to his own things, but each of you also to the things of others...

"Be tenderly affectioned one to another, in honor preferring one another....

"Judge not that ye be not judged.... The rich and the poor meet together: Jehovah is the maker of them all....

"Better it is to be of a lowly spirit....

"He that is slow in anger appeaseth strife....

"I am among you as he that serveth....

"Ye are the light of the world...."

The best book for anyone who is trying to be a success in the world is the Bible, for the Bible teaches how to serve, and he who has the courage best to serve his fellows in the name of the great Servant is the most successful man.

III
SERVICE BY SYMPATHY

It has been said that, while the word "sympathy" does not occur in the Bible, the idea is there; it is in bud in the Old Testament, but it is in full blossom in the New Testament. Christ was always sympathetic. He felt for the disturbed host at the wedding; His heart went out to Zaccheus; He wept with Mary and Martha; He listened to the plea of the blind and the lepers; He was deeply stirred as He saw the funeral procession of him who was the only son of his mother, a widow.

An eloquent preacher was talking to his people of this glorious flower of the Christian life. "Beholding the lily," he said, "sympathy breathes a prayer that no untimely frost may blight the blossom; beholding the sparrow, sympathy fills a box with seeds for the birds whose fall 'the Heavenly Father knoweth'; beholding some youth going forth to make his fortune, sympathy prays that favorable winds may fill these sails and waft the boy to fame and fortune. Do the happy youth and maiden stand before the marriage altar, the Christian breathes a prayer that love's flowers may never fall, and that 'those who are now young may grow old together.'"

One of the pleasing stories told of Richard Harding Davis, the writer and war correspondent, was of an incident when real sympathy transformed him.

In May, 1898, when the Massachusetts troops were about to go from Florida to Cuba, Mr. Davis entered the encampment as the men were saddened by the first death in the company. At once his cheerful face took on a subdued look. The next day proved to be "a broiling dry hot day which set the blood sizzling inside of one," but Davis tramped for two hours in the search of flowers. Then he learned that eight miles away he might secure some. Though no one was abroad who did not have to be, Mr. Davis started on a sixteen-mile horseback trip. Securing the flowers, he brought them back and made a cross of laths on which he tied them. Then came the search for colors to make the flag. Again he tramped a weary distance, but at last he found red, white and blue ribbon. That night he laid his tribute on the casket.

An American author who lived several generations before Davis was noted for his sympathetic attitude to the suffering. Richard Henry Dana was compelled when a young man to take a voyage around Cape Horn on a sailing ship. That classic of the sea, "Two Years Before the Mast," was one of the results of that experience. Another result was that when the author became a lawyer in Boston, his knowledge of ships made him a favorite advocate in nautical cases. His knowledge of the sufferings of the men before the mast, who were so often abused, was responsible for his taking their part in many an unprofitable case. He had learned by bitter experience what the sailors under a brutal captain had to suffer, and any mistreated seaman had in him a firm friend and a fearless pleader.

The truest sympathy comes from those who, like Dana, know what suffering means. An author in Scotland, who lived in Dana's generation, never heard of the American friend of seamen, but he had the same spirit, born of his own suffering. He was not accustomed to complain, and was always reticent in speaking of himself. Once, however, for the sake of a friend, he allowed himself to tell of his own life:

"With all your sorrows I sympathize from my heart," he wrote. "I have learned to do so through my own sufferings. The same feeling which made you put your hand into your pocket to search among the crumbs for the wanting coin for the beggar, leads me to search in my heart for some consolation for you. The last two years have been fraught to me with such sorrowful experiences that I would gladly exchange my condition for a peaceful grave. A bankrupt in health, hope and fortune, my constitution shattered frightfully, and the almost certain prospect of being a cripple for life before me, I can offer you as fervent and unselfish a sympathy as ever one heart offered another. I have lain awake, alone, and in darkness, suffering severe agony for hours, often thinking that the slightest aggravation must make my condition unbearable and finding my only consolation in murmuring to myself the words patience, courage and submission."

That, surely, is a part of what Robert Louis Stevenson meant when, as one element in his statement of the ideal for the perfect life, he named "to be kind." True kindness is impossible without sympathy.

So long as there is so much real sympathy in the world there can be no place for the maunderings of a pessimist. Every sight of a man, a woman or a child whose life is beautified by the outgoing of sympathy is an effective message of courage, of cheer, of hope.

IV
DOING BUSINESS FOR OTHERS

A Boston boy, Samuel Billings Capen, wanted to become a minister. Yet it did not seem possible to secure the special training which was essential. Instead of being discouraged, he determined to go into business.

But he resolved that he would be a business man of God. From the first he carried his Christian principles with him into the carpet business. His faithful work as office boy was a part of his testimony for Christ, and when—within five years—he became a member of the firm, he was known as one of the solid Christian men of the city. Always his duty to Christ came first. In the words of his biographer, "There was not a moment when he would not have left the firm with which he was associated had the business demanded any compromise with the best things of character."

Once he spoke to young men of these few things essential to vital living:

"The first is fidelity—that kind of conscientiousness which performs the smallest details well.

"The second condition is earnestness. There is no chance for the idle or indifferent.

"The third condition is integrity—not that lower form which refuses to tell a downright falsehood, but that higher form of conscientiousness which will not swerve a hair's breadth from the strictest truth, no matter what the temptation; the courage to lose a sale rather than to do that which is mean or questionable.

"The fourth condition I would name is purity of heart and life. I do not believe it is possible for any man to be true and pure and faithful in every respect without help from above. We need the personal help of a personal God."

Thirteen years after beginning his service as apprentice, Mr. Capen's health failed. For many months his life was in danger. God used the sickness to draw the young man nearer to Himself. "Compelled to remain for months in absolute idleness, unable to talk to his friends except to a limited extent, he made the solemn resolve with his God that if his health was restored he would never shirk any work nor complain of any task that might be presented to him."

For a generation he was not only a leader in business, but he was as conspicuous in his service of the State as in his services in the Church.

Why did he succeed? He was not a genius. His health was poor. He was not mentally brilliant. In these respects he was just an average man. But in other respects he was above the average. He had the courage to give himself in service of his fellows. "He believed that conscious fellowship with God is the foundation of every strong life."

A life like that influenced for good everyone about him. Many men were drawn by him into the paths of righteousness. Others were held back by him from ways of evil. Once he presided over a public meeting which corrupt politicians had planned to capture for their own purpose. But they made no attempt to carry out their plans. "How could we succeed with that man watching us?" they asked their friends.

It is good to be a minister of the gospel. But for every minister the world needs hundreds of men who are possessed of Samuel B. Capen's courageous eagerness to live for God in the midst of business cares.

V
PRAYING AND HELPING

A business man entered the office of a friend just as the friend was hanging up the receiver of the telephone. There were tears in the eyes of the man at the desk as he turned from the instrument to take the hand of his visitor.

"I'm afraid you have had bad news," the visitor said, deciding that it was not a propitious time to talk of the matter on which he had come.

"No bad news—the best of news," was the reply. "Now see if you don't agree with me. This morning my wife, who is always thinking of other people, remarked that it was too bad my pastor's wife could not have a vacation this summer; she shows the need of it because of a severe strain that had been on her. Yet we knew that she could not look forward to a vacation.

"'Let's pray about it,' my wife suggested, just before we knelt at the family altar. We prayed then; we've been praying since. And the answer has come quickly. My wife was on the telephone just now; she told me that the postman had brought a letter from a California friend of whom we had all but lost sight. Fifteen years ago we lent him a sum of money which we never expected to see again. Yet the letter contained a check for the amount of the loan!

"'What shall we do with the money?' my wife asked.

"'I wonder if you are not thinking the same thing I am,' I said to her.

"'Yes, isn't it the answer to our prayer?' she replied. 'I'm going to take it to our pastor's wife right now.'"

The business man was thoughtful as he passed from his friend's office. Just a few hours before he had been told by an acquaintance of his longing, when on a long trip, to have such a glimpse of the life of one of the many passengers near him that he would be able to help that passenger before the end of the journey. The wish was a prayer. Not long after the making of the prayer he noted a man who was so restless that he could not sit still. Every moment or two he looked at his watch, then studied his time table. Evidently he was disturbed because the train was late.

"I hope you are not to lose a connection in Chicago?" the observing traveler said to him.

"Yes, I'll miss it—and my baby is dying five hours from Chicago," was the response, given with a sob.

The time was short, but there was opportunity for the interchange of a few words, then for a conference with the conductor, who wired asking that the connecting train—at another station and on another road—be held for ten minutes.

A week later came a note from the happy father. His babe was rapidly recovering. "And I'll never forget the words you spoke to me in my agony," he wrote. "God is more real to me since our talk as we went into Chicago. You put heart into me."

VI
GIVING THAT COUNTS

An old fable tells of a good man to whom the Lord said he would give whatever he most desired. Besought by friends to ask great things, he refused. Finally he asked that he might be able to do a great deal of good without ever knowing it. And so it came about that every time the good man's shadow fell behind him or at either side, so that he could not see it, it had the power to cure disease, soothe pain and comfort sorrow.

When he walked along, his shadow, thrown on the ground on either side or behind him, made arid paths green, caused withered plants to bloom, gave clear water to dried up brooks, fresh color to pale little children, and joy to unhappy mothers.

But he simply went about his daily life, diffusing virtue as the star diffuses light and the flower perfume, without ever being aware of it. And the people, respecting his humility, followed him silently, never speaking to him about his miracles. Little by little, they even came to forget his name, and called him only "The Holy Shadow."

It would be a splendid thing if all would learn the lesson taught in the fable—that the man who would do good should have the courage to be unconscious of the good he is doing, and so as unlike as possible the rich woman of whom some one has told, who turned a deaf ear to every petition for help unless there was a subscription paper circulated and she was given the chance to head the list. "But no poor person came into her house who said, 'May God reward you!' She never experienced the pleasure of making a poor woman on the back stairs happy with a cup of warm coffee, or hungry children with a slice of bread and butter, or an infirm man with a penny. Perhaps she satisfied her conscience by saying that she did not believe in indiscriminate charity. Frequently that excuse is given conscientiously but how often the real meaning is, 'I do not believe in charity that does not make people talk of my generosity.'"

In the Sermon on the Mount Jesus taught the folly of giving in such a manner. The lesson was enforced by two pictures—a man standing on the street, giving alms to the poor, while attention is called to his generosity by the sounding of a trumpet which everyone must hear, and a man whose giving is so much a matter of secrecy that he does not think of it a second time. There is no rolling of it over as a sweetmeat under his tongue, as if to say, "What a generous man I am!" Nor is there any motive in the giving but pure desire to glorify God. All this is properly included in the interpretation of "Let not thy left hand know what thy right hand doeth."

VII
EXPENSIVE ECONOMY

A magazine editor offered a prize for the best account by a reader of the adjustment of income and expenditure made necessary by the vaulting prices of recent years. The prize was awarded to one whose revised budget showed the revision downward of many items, and the elimination of two or three other items. The comparison of the budgets was interesting and helpful; most readers would be apt to approve heartily all but one of the changes and eliminations. This was the exception: the earlier budget allowed five dollars per month for "church and charity," while the revised budget made no mention of the claims of others, no provision for the privilege of giving.

If you had been a judge in that contest, would you have felt like giving the prize to a paper that suggested such an omission? Suppose you had the task of cutting your budget, would you feel like revising downward the provision for giving? What do you think of the statement of a famous business man who, having insisted in time of financial reverses on making gifts as usual, said to objecting friends, "Economy should not begin at the house of God." Why not let economy begin there?

What answer would have been given to such a query by the poor tenement dweller in New York City who, though compelled to earn the support of her family by scrubbing floors in a great office building, set aside a dollar and a half per week for the care of four orphans in India who but for her gifts would have starved?

What answer would have been made by the Polish Jew, long resident in America, who directed in his will that regular gifts be made at Christmas and Easter to the Christians as well as to the Jews of his home town in Europe? That bequest was made in memory of days and nights of terror when, as a boy, he hid in the house from the fiendish persecutions of so-called Christians who thought Easter and Christmas favorable times for the intimidation of the Jews. What would he have said to the idea of economy that forgets the needs of others and makes no provision for satisfying the hungry, to help the suffering?

What would have been the comment of Him who told the parable of the rich man who built great barns to hold the surplus product of his lands, thinking that there was nothing better in life than to eat, drink, and be merry; who compared the gifts of the rich man and the poor widow; who commended the love of the woman who poured out the costly ointment upon His head; who promises glorious recognition to those who give, in His name, to any who are in need?

A successful manufacturer, whose eyes have been opened to the folly of attempting to save by cutting off gifts, has written a series of essays on "The Business Man and His Overflow," his purpose being to show that happiness is dependent on helpfulness. "Who is the most successful business man?" he asks. "The man who has the largest bank account? Not necessarily. . . . The most successful business man is he who renders the greatest service to mankind and whose life is most useful."

Two paths are open to us: we can give, and we can give more, or we can economize in giving until we give nothing.

Which is the path of courage?

CHAPTER SEVEN

COURAGE THROUGH COMPANIONSHIP

THE world is full of lonely people—people who keep to themselves, turning away from every approach of others, from all invitations to come out of retirement. They persist in living alone, thinking their own thoughts, pleasing only themselves.

"I can have no place in my life for friendship," one of these unfortunates says.

"I can't be expected to devote myself to my family; it is all I can do to make a living," is the complaint of another.

"I live in the present," says a third; "the past has no interest for me, and the future holds nothing but worries."

"Live more out-of-doors, you say!" is the word of a fourth. "Why should I bother about Nature when Nature does nothing but thwart me?"

"Make God my friend?" a fifth asks in surprise. "Talk to me in rational terms. God doesn't bother about me; why should I bother about Him?"

Is it any wonder that the lives of so many everywhere are empty? It does not occur to them that by their determination to isolate themselves they cut themselves off from the surest road to courage, both received and given— the road of companionship with the people and things most worth while.

I
COMPANIONSHIP WITH FRIENDS

There are those who say that friendship is a lost art; that modern life is too busy for friendship. "Why don't you pause long enough to call on B——?" a father asked his son; "you used to be such good friends." "Oh, I haven't time for that now," was the careless reply; "if I am to get ahead, I feel I must devote myself only to those things that can be a decided help to my advancement."

The mistake made by that son is emphasized by the advice of a keen old man, spoken to a business associate: "If I were asked to give advice to a group of young men who wanted to get ahead in business, I would simply say, 'make friends.' As I sat before the fire the other night I let my mind run back, and it was with surprise that I learned that many of the things which in my youth I credited to my ability as a business man came to me because I had made influential friends who did things for me because they liked me. The man who is right has the right kind of friends, and the man who is wrong has the kind of friends who are attracted by his wrongness. A man gets what he is."

Possibly some will think that advice faulty in expression, for it seems at first glance to put friendship on a coldly calculating basis, as if it urged the maker of friends to say before consenting to try for a man's friendship, "Is there anything I can get out of such a friendship for myself?" Of course it is unthinkable that anyone should estimate friendship in that way; friendship that calculates is unworthy the name, and the calculator ought to be doomed to the loneliest kind of life. But, evidently, what the adviser had in mind is the spirit that makes friends because it is worth while to have friends for friendship's sake, that never counts on advancement through the efforts of others. Such a spirit is bound to be surprised some day by the realization that for his success he owed much to the friends whom he made without a thought of self.

One beginner in business decided that he must find his friendships in serving others. There were those who told him he was making a mistake, but he went calmly on, devoting hours each week to service with an associate in a boys' club. Nothing seemed to come of this but satisfaction to himself and joy to a group whose homes were cheerless. Yet, there was something more—the pleasure of friendship with his associate. One day he was surprised by an invitation to call on the head of a large manufacturing concern. "You don't know me," the man said, "but I know you, for you have been teaching with my son down at the boys' club. For a long time I have been on the lookout for a young man who can come into this business with a view to taking up the work with my son when I must retire. From what I have heard your friend, my son, tell of you, you are the man I have sought."

It is impossible to count on a thing like that as a result of friendship, and the man who is worthy of such a friendship never thinks of reckoning on anything but giving to his friend the best that is in him as he enjoys the comfort of association with him.

Many years ago the author of *The Four Feathers* wrote of such a friendship between two men:

"It was a helpful instrument, which would not wear out, put into their hands for a hard, lifelong use, but it was not and never had been spoken of between them. Both men were grateful for it, as for a rare and undeserved gift; yet both knew that it might entail an obligation of sacrifice. But the sacrifices, were they needful, would be made, and they would not be mentioned."

It has been well said that "Love gives and receives, and keeps no account on either side," but that is very different from deliberately using friendship for selfish ends.

II
SUCCESSFUL COMRADES

For days two men had been together, tramping, driving, boating, eating, sleeping, talking. And when the time for separation came, one said to the other: "Will you please give a message to your wife? Tell her for me, if you will, that she has made her husband into a real comrade."

That man would have been at a loss to tell what are the elements that go to the making up of a good comrade. In fact, he intimated as much on the last day of the excursion. "You can no more tell the things that go to make up a real comrade than you can explain the things that make a landscape beautiful; you can only see and rejoice."

Just so, it is possible to see instances of good comradeship and rejoice.

In order that there may be real comradeship between two individuals it is not at all necessary that they shall belong to the same station in life. One of those to whom John Muir, the great naturalist, proved himself a true comrade was a guide who many times went with him into the fastnesses of the high Sierras of California. "It was great to hear him talk," the guide has said. "Often we sat together like two men who had always known each other. It wasn't always necessary to talk; often there would be no word said for half an hour. But we understood each other in the silence."

Nor is it essential that people shall be much together before they can be real comrades. Theodore Roosevelt and Joel Chandler Harris knew one another by reputation only until the red letter day when Uncle Remus entered the door of the White House, in response to an urgent letter of invitation in which the President wrote: "Presidents may come and presidents may go, but Uncle Remus stays put. Georgia has done a great many things for the Union, but she has never done more than when she gave Joel Chandler Harris to American literature." When the two animal-lovers finally came together there was real comradeship. That the reporters understood this was evident from the wire one of them sent to his paper: "Midnight—Mr. Harris has not returned to his hotel. The White House is ablaze with light. It is said that Mr. Harris is telling the story of Br'er Rabbit and the Tar Baby." But the Georgian's own colloquial account of the memorable session with his comrade at Washington was more explicit:

"There are things about the White House that'll astonish you ef ever you git there while Teddy is on hand. It's a home; it'll come over you like a sweet dream the minnit you git in the door. . . . It's a kind of feelin' that you kin have in your own house, if you've lived right, but it's the rarest thing in the world that you kin find it in anybody else's house. . . . We mostly talked of little children an' all the pranks they're up to from mornin' till night, an' how they draw old folks into all sorts of traps, and make 'em play tricks on themselves. That's the kinder talk I like, an' I could set up long past my bedtime an' listen to it. Jest at the right time, the President would chip in wi' some of his adventures wi' the children. . . . I felt just like I had been on a visit to some old friend that I hadn't seen in years."

When Robert Louis Stevenson and Edward Livingston Trudeau spent days together at Dr. Trudeau's Adirondack sanitarium—the one as patient, the other as physician—they proved that true comradeship is possible even when men's tastes are most unlike. It was possible because they knew how to ignore differences and to find common ground in the worth-while things. "My life interests were bound up in the study of facts, and in the laboratory I bowed duly to the majesty of fact, wherever it might lead," Dr. Trudeau wrote. "Mr. Stevenson's view was to ignore or avoid as much as possible unpleasant facts, and live in a beautiful, extraneous and ideal world of fancy. I got him one day into the laboratory, from which he escaped at the first opportunity. . . . On the other hand, I knew well I could not discuss intelligently with him the things he lived among and the masterly work he produced, because I was incompetent to appreciate to the full the wonderful situations his brilliant mind evolved and the high literary merit of the work in which he described the flights of his great genius."

Yet these two men were great companions, for in spite of differences as to details, their hopes and ambitions and ideals all pointed to the best things in life. After the author's departure, he sent to the doctor a splendidly bound set of his works, first writing in each volume a whimsical bit of rhyme, composed for the occasion.

Though all of these men were real comrades, there is a higher manifestation of comradeship than this. This was shown in the relation of Daniel Coit Gilman, later President of Johns Hopkins University, when he wrote to a fellow student of the deepest things in his life:

"I don't wish merely to thank you in a general way for writing as you did an expression of sympathy, but more especially to respond to the sentiments on Christian acquaintance which you there bring out. I agree with you most fully and only regret that I did not know at an earlier time upon our journey what were your feelings upon a few such topics. I tell you, Brace, that I hate cant and all that sort of thing as much as you or anyone else can do. It is not with everyone that I would enjoy a talk upon religious subjects. I hardly ever wrote a letter on them to those I know best. But when anyone believes in an inner life of faith and joy, and is willing to talk about it in an earnest, everyday style and tone, I do enjoy it most exceedingly."

Theodore Storrs Lee cultivated the relation of a comrade with his fellow students that he might talk to them, without cant, on the deepest things of life. His biographer says: "Many a time did he seek out men in lonely rooms, bewildered or weakened by the college struggles. Many a quiet talk did he have as he and his selected companion trod his favorite walk. No one else in college had so many intimate talks with so many men. . . . On one occasion, when he was urging a friend to give his life to Christian service, he seemed to be unsuccessful—until, on leaving the man at the close of the walk, he made a genial, large-minded remark that opened the way to the heart of his friend." . . . "It was only natural that I should try to meet him half-way," the friend said later, in explanation of his own changed attitude. He had been won by real comradeliness. "It was this devotion to the men in college that led him into the holy of holies of many a man's heart," wrote a friend, "causing many of us to feel in a very real way the sentiment expressed by Mrs. Browning:

> "The face of all the world is changed, I think
> Since first I heard the footsteps of thy soul."

III
COMPANIONSHIP WITH THE PAST

What, courage from companionship with the past? The pessimist says, "Impossible! The past was so much better than the present. See how the country is going to the dogs!" and they point to the revelations of dishonesty in high places. "There were no such blots on our records when the country was young."

A public man gave an effective answer to such croakers when he said:

"As we go on year by year reading in the newspapers of the dreadful things that are occurring; wicked rich men, wicked politicians and wicked men of all kinds, we are apt to feel that we have fallen on very evil times. But are we any worse than our fathers were? John Adams, in 1776, was Secretary of War. He wrote a letter which is still in existence, and told of the terrible corruption that prevailed in the country; he told how everybody was trying to rob the soldiers, rob the War Department, and he said he was really ashamed of the times in which he lived. When Jefferson was President of the United States it was thought that the whole country was going to be given over to French infidelity. When Jackson was President people thought the country ruined, because of his action in regard to the United States Bank. And we know how in Polk's time the Mexican War was an era of rascality and dishonesty that appalled the whole country."

It is a mistake to look back a generation or two and say, "The good old days were better than these." In the address already referred to the speaker continued:

"Only thirty years ago, on my first visit to California, I went with a friend to the mining district in the Sierras. One summer evening we sat upon the flume looking over the landscape. My friend was a distinguished man of great ability. In the distance the sun was setting, reflecting its light on the dome of the Capitol of the state, at Sacramento, twenty miles off. He turned to me and said suddenly: 'I would like to be you for one reason, that you are thirty years younger than I am, and they are going to be thirty of the greatest years the world has ever seen.' He is dead now, but his words were prophetic. He and I used to talk about how we could send power down into the mines. An engine would fill the mine with smoke and gases, and yet we must have power to run the drills, etc., using compressed air. How easy to-day, just to drop a wire down and send the power of electricity! At that time there was but a single railroad running across the continent, which took a single sleeping car each day. Look at the difference now, with six great trunk lines sending out more than a dozen trains, and more than a hundred sleeping cars each day."

Students of American history know something of the fears of early adherents of the United States Government lest the republic prove a failure, and of the threats of doubters and disaffected citizens to do their best to replace the republic by a monarchy. But comparatively few realize how great were the fears, and how brazenly the prophecies were spoken.

An examination of "The Complete Anas of Thomas Jefferson," the collection of private memoranda made by the patriot when he was successively Secretary of State, Vice-President, and President, discloses the fact that some of the gravest of these fears were held by those high in authority, and that the prophecies of evil came from men who were leaders in the nation.

On April 6, 1792, President Washington, in conversation with Jefferson, "expressed his fear that there would, ere long, be a separation of the Union, that the public mind seemed dissatisfied and tending to this." On October 1, 1792, he spoke to the Secretary of his desire to retire at the end of his term as President. "Still, however, if his aid was thought necessary to save the cause to which he had devoted his life principally, he would make the sacrifice of a longer continuance."

On April 7, 1793, Tobias Lear, in conversation with Jefferson, spoke pessimistically of the affairs of the country. The debt, he was sure, was growing on the country in spite of claims to the contrary. He said that "the man who vaunted the present government so much on some occasions was the very man who at other times declared that it was a poor thing, and such a one as could not stand, and he was sensible they only esteemed it as a stepping-stone to something else."

On December 1, 1793, an influential Senator (name given) said to several of his fellow Senators that things would never go right until there was a President for life, and a hereditary Senate.

On December 27, 1797, Jefferson said that Tenche Coxe told him that a little before Alexander Hamilton went out of office, he said: "For my part I avow myself a monarchist; I have no objection to a trial being made of this thing of a republic, but, . . . etc."

On February 6, 1798, it was reported to Jefferson that a man of influence in the Government had said, "I have made up my mind on this subject; I would rather the old ship should go down than not." Later he qualified his words, making his statement hypothetical, by adding, "if we are to be always kept pumping so."

On January 24, 1800, it was reported to Jefferson that, at a banquet in New York, Alexander Hamilton made no remark when the health of the President was proposed, but that he asked for three cheers when the health of George III was suggested.

On March 27, 1800, the Anas record: "Dr. Rush tells me that within a few days he has heard a member of Congress lament our separation from

Great Britain, and express his sincere wishes that we were again dependent on her."

On December 13, 1803, Jefferson told of the coming to President Adams of a minister from New England who planned to solicit funds in New England for a college in Green County, Tennessee. He wished to have the President's endorsement of the project. But "Mr. Adams . . . said he saw no possibility of continuing the union of the States; that their dissolution must take place; that he therefore saw no propriety in recommending to New England men to promote a literary institution in the South; that it was in fact giving strength to those who were to be their enemies, and, therefore, he would have nothing to do with it."

One who reads bits like these from Jefferson's private papers appreciates more fully some of the grave difficulties that confronted the country's early leaders; he rejoices more than ever before that the United States emerged so triumphantly from troubled waters until, little more than a century after those days of dire foreboding, it was showing other nations the way to democracy; he takes courage in days of present doubt and uncertainty, assured that the country which has already weathered so many storms will continue to solve its grave problems, and will be more than ever a beacon light to the world.

IV
COMPANIONSHIP WITH NATURE

"Look at the World," is the advice David Grayson gives to those who follow him in his delightful essays on Great Possessions—possessions that cannot be measured with a yardstick or entered in the bank book. This is his cure for all the trials and vexations that come in the course of a busy life. For how can a man remain unsettled and morose and distressed when he is gazing at the broad expanse of the sky, studying the beauty of the trees, or listening to the mellow voices of the birds? How can the wanderer in field and forest forget that God is love?

Some people think that to drink in the glories of nature they must go to the mountains, or seek some other far-away spot. Mistake! The place to enjoy God's world is just where one is, and the time is that very moment.

This was the lesson taught so impressively by Alice Freeman Palmer, when she described the little dweller in the tenements who resolved to see something beautiful each day, and who, one day, when confined to the house, found her something in watching a rain-soaked sparrow drinking from the gutter on the tin roof. And this was the thought in the mind of Mr. Grayson when he said:

"I love a sprig of white cedar, especially the spicy, sweet inside bark, or a pine needle, or the tender, sweet, juicy end of a spike of timothy grass drawn slowly from its sheath, or a twig of the birch that tastes like wintergreen."

Hamlin Garland, in "A Son of the Middle Border," has told the story of his boyhood on an Iowa farm. He knew how to enjoy the sights to which so many are blind:

"I am reliving days when the warm sun, falling on radiant slopes of grass, lit the meadow phlox and tall tiger lilies to flaming torches of color. I think of blackberry thickets and odorous grapevines, and cherry-trees and the delicious nuts which grew in profusion throughout the forest to the north. The forest, which seemed endless and was of enchanted solemnity, served as our wilderness. We explored it at every opportunity. We loved every day for the color it brought, each season for the wealth of its experiences, and we welcomed the thought of spending all our years in this beautiful home where the wood and the prairie of our song did actually meet and mingle. . . . I studied the clouds. I gnawed the beautiful red skin from the seed vessels which hung upon the wild rose bushes, and I counted the prairie chickens as they began to come together in winter flocks, running through the stubble in search of food. I stopped now and again to examine the lizards unhoused by the shares, . . . and I measured the little granaries of wheat which the mice and gophers had deposited deep under the ground, storehouses which the plow had violated. My eyes dwelt enviously on the sailing hawk and on the passing of ducks. . . . Often of a warm day I heard the sovereign cry of the sand-hill crane falling from the azure throne, so high, so far, his form could not be seen, so close to the sun that my eyes could not detect his solitary, majestic, circling sweep. . . . His brazen, reverberating call will forever remain associated in my mind with mellow, pulsating earth, spring grass and cloudless glorious May-time skies."

Henry Fawcett lived at about the same period in a rural district in England. He, too, delighted to ramble in the fields. One day, when he was out hunting with his father, an accidental gunshot deprived him of his eyesight. But the boy would not think of shutting himself away from the joys of nature which meant so much to him. "I very soon came to the resolution to live, as far as possible, just as I had lived before. . . . No one can more enjoy catching a salmon in the Tweed of the Spey, or throwing a fly in some quiet trout stream in Wiltshire or Hampshire."

In the story of the life of John J. Audubon an incident is told that shows how the greatest joy can be found in what seems like one of the most ordinary things in the life of the forest—the nesting of the birds:

"He became interested in a bird, not as large as the wren, of such peculiar grey plumage that it harmonized with the bark of the trees, and could scarcely be seen. One night he came home greatly excited, saying he had found a pair that was evidently preparing to make a nest. The next morning he went into the woods, taking with him a telescopic microscope. The scientific instrument he erected under the tree that gave shelter to the literally invisible inhabitants he was searching for, and, making a pillow of some moss, he lay upon his back, and looking through the telescope, day after day, noted the progress of the little birds, and, after three weeks of such patient labor, felt that he had been amply rewarded for the toil and the sacrifice by the results he had obtained."

When a boy David Livingstone laid the foundation for the love of the open that helped to make his life in Africa a never-ending delight. "Before he was ten he had wandered all over the Clyde banks about Blantyre and had begun to collect and wonder at shells and flowers," one of his biographers says.

Not far away, also in Scotland, Henry Drummond spent his boyhood. He, too, knew the pleasure of wandering afield. He liked to go to the rock on which stands grim Stirling Castle, and look away to the windings of the crooked Forth, the green Ochil Hills, and, farther away, Ben Lomond, Ben Venue, and Ben Ledi, the guardians of the beautiful Highland lochs. He was never weary of feasting his eyes on them. In later years he would go back to the scenes of his boyhood, climb to the Castle, and, looking out on the beautiful prospect, would say "Man, there's no place like this; no place like Scotland."

Bayard Taylor first made a name for himself by his ability to see the things that many people pass by, and to describe them sympathetically. But he, also, in boyhood days learned the lesson that paved the way for later achievements. He was not six years old when he used to wander to a fascinating swamp near his Pennsylvania home. If the child was missed from the house, the first thing that suggested itself was to climb upon a mound which overlooked the swamp. Once, from the roof of the house, he discovered unknown forests and fresh fields which he made up his mind to explore. Later, in company with a Quaker schoolmaster, he took long walks, and thus learned many things about the trees and plants. When he was twelve he began to write out the thoughts that came to him in this intimate study of nature.

In far-away Norway Ole Bull had a like experience. At an early age he began to be on familiar terms with the silent things about him. The quality of his later work was influenced by the grandeur of the scenery in which he lived. To him trees, rocks, waterfalls, mountains, all spoke a language which demanded expression through the strings of his violin; he turned everything into music. His biographer says:

"When, in early childhood, playing alone in the meadow, he saw a delicate bluebell moving in the breeze, he fancied he heard the bell ring, and the grass accompanying it with most exceptionally fine voices."

John Muir, who later wrote of the great Sequoias of California and the glaciers of Alaska, when a boy of ten found delight in scenes of which he wrote as follows:

"Oh, that glorious Wisconsin wilderness! Everything new and pure in the very prime of spring, when nature's pulses were beating highest and mysteriously keeping tune with our own! Young hearts, young leaves, flowers, animals, the winds and the streams and the sparkling lake, all wildly, gladly rejoicing together."

There is something missing in the life of one who cannot enter into the feelings of a boy like Muir or Taylor or Drummond. And when such a boy grows up, the gap in the life will be more conspicuous than ever.

Think of the poverty of the stranger to whom a traveler, feeling that he must give expression to his keen delight in the autumn foliage, said, "What wonderful coloring!" "Where?" came the reply. "Oh, the trees! Well, I'm not interested in trees. Talk to me about coal. I know coal."

V
COMPANIONSHIP WITH GOD

Some people insist that it is impractical moonshine to speak of making a companion of God, that folks who talk about such things are dreamers, far removed from touch with the cold reality of daily life.

Then how about the nephew of whom Dr. Alexander MacColl told at Northfield? He was surely a practical man. For four years he had been in the thick of the fighting in France. Yet at the close of one of his letters to his uncle he said: "I hope when the war is over that I may be able to spend a month somewhere among the hills. I often think that if more people in the world had lived among such hills as we have in Scotland there would have been no world war."

"When I came yesterday afternoon, and saw again the glory of these hills," was Dr. MacColl's comment, "I found myself sharing very deeply in that feeling of my good nephew, and wishing that more people in the world had known what it is to commune with God in the silences."

That fine young Scotchman would have known how to take a college student who, while having a country walk with a friend, was explaining the reason for his belief in God and his trust in Him. As he concluded his message he pointed to a large tree which they were passing, saying as he did so, "God is as real to me as that tree."

He had a right to say such a thing, for he not only believed, but he was conscious that God was with him, his Companion wherever he went. This being the case, prayer became for him the simplest and most natural thing in the world. God was by his side; then why should not he talk to God, by ejaculation as well as by more formal utterance? Yet his talks with God never became formal. They were always intimate and confidential—like the approaches of Principal John Cairns, the famous Scotch minister. His biographer tells of a time when he was at the manse of a country minister in whose church he was to preach next day. The minister's wife withdrew to get a cup of tea for the old man, leaving her little boy there. By and by she heard a strange, unaccustomed sound, as it seemed to her under such conditions. And as she listened and looked, she saw that the old man was kneeling with the boy. It had seemed to him the most natural thing in the world to speak to his Great Friend about his little friend.

Dr. Arthur Smith was like that with God, and his son Henry took after him. One January day in 1905 the father reached New York from China and sought his son. They went to a hotel room to bridge the time of absence by "a tremendous lot of back conversation," as the son wrote to the mother. But before they had any chance to talk of other matters the father said, "Come, boy, let's have a prayer." "Wasn't that just like him?" Henry asked his mother.

A minister who was spending his vacation in the northern woods was called in to see a dying lumberman. Before leaving the visitor prayed with the sick man, and suggested that he pray for himself. The objection was made that it was useless to pray—God understood a man's trials, and He knew what was wanted before a request was made. The minister asked him if he didn't know what his children needed before they asked him, if he didn't know they were disappointed or troubled; yet didn't he wish to have them talk over these things with him?

The man thought a moment. Then he said, "Do you think that would be prayer—just for me to lie here and tell God what He knows already—how it hurts, and all my disappointment, and my anxiety for the future of my children and my wife—and everything—just to tell Him?"

"I think it would," said the minister. "I think it would be prayer of a very real kind."

One who had learned that prayer is not a mere formal exercise, to be dreaded and postponed, has said:

"Pray often—in bits, with a persistency of habit that betrays a childlike eagerness and absorption. Rise up to question God as children do their earthly parents—at morning, noon and night and between times. Ask Him about everything. Be with Him more than with all other persons. Acquire the home habit with Him. Be a child in His hands. Do not fear lest He be too busy to listen, or too grown up to care or to understand. Just talk to Him, in broken sentences, half-formed with crude wishes; in foolish chatter, if need be. Make the Heavenly Father the center of your life, the source and judge of all your satisfactions. Be sure to let Him put you to bed, waken you in the morning, wait on you at table, order your day's doings, protect you from harm, soothe your disquiet, supply all your daily needs."

Such a prayer is good, not only when one is sick, but when one is well and busy with the affairs of daily life. A clergyman has told of a visit to London during which he called on a merchant whom he had met in America. At the business house he was told that he could not see the merchant, as it was steamer day, and orders had been given not to disturb him. But when the card was taken up, the merchant appeared, his face beaming with pleasure. After a moment's greeting the visitor offered to go away, but the merchant took him into his office, and said:

"I am very glad you have called. I would not have had you fail. I am very busy, but I always have a moment for my Lord. I have a little place for private prayer. You must come in with me, and we shall have a season of prayer together."

Busy, but not too busy for prayer, longing to see his friend, but eager to spend the ten minutes of the call in prayer with that other Friend who made the brief visit worth while!

In telling this incident, one writer on the subject of prayer has said:

"Several, perhaps many merchants in one of our large cities have fitted up for themselves dark, narrow, boxlike closets, whither, each by himself, they are wont to retire for a few minutes at times, during the pressure of the day's business, for the refreshment of soul, which they find they really need in communion with God. One of these men is reported to have said: 'On some days, if I had not that resort, I believe I should go mad, so great is the pressure.'"

Dr. Purves once told an incident of the distinguished scientist, Professor Joseph Henry, as given him by one of Dr. Henry's students. "I well remember the wonderful care with which he arranged all his principal experiments. Then often, when the testing moment came, that holy as well as great philosopher would raise his hand in adoring reverence and call upon me to uncover my head and worship in silence, 'because,' he said, 'God is here. I am about to ask God a question.'"

To Mary Slessor of Calabar, whom the Africans learned to love devotedly, prayer was as simple and easy as talking to a friend in the room. "Her religion was a religion of the heart," her biographer says. "Her communion with her Father was of the most natural, most childlike character. No rule or habit guided her. She just spoke to Him as a child to its father when she needed help and strength, or when her heart was filled with joy and gratitude, at any time, in any place. He was so real to her, so near, that her words were almost of the nature of conversation. There was no formality, no self-consciousness, no stereotyped diction, only the simplest language from a quiet and humble heart. It is told of her that once, when she was in Scotland, after a tiresome journey, she sat down at the tea table alone, and, lifting up her eyes, said, 'Thank you, Father—ye ken I'm tired,' in the most ordinary way as if she had been addressing her friend. On another occasion in the country, she lost her spectacles while coming from a meeting in the dark. She could not do without them, and she prayed simply and directly, 'O Father, give me back my spectacles!' A lady asked her how she obtained such intimacy with God. 'Ah, woman,' she said, 'when I am out there in the bush, I have often no other one to speak to but my Father, and I just talk to Him. . . .'"

"I just talk to Him!" There is the secret of getting and keeping close to the Father, the most worth-while Companion we can possibly have with us on country walk, on vacation excursion, amid business perplexities, in the desert or in the thronged city street, when the days are crowded with burdens, or when the time of rest after work has come.

Try Him and see if it is not so.

A CHAPTER OF—ACCIDENTS?

A man had planned a three-day trip with care. On paper everything looked promising for a combination of business and pleasure that would make these days stand out in the record of the year.

In the morning he would go to Washington. There he would have opportunity to see in one of the Departments a man whose help in an emergency would prove invaluable. At four in the afternoon he would leave for Cincinnati. By taking the train he would miss a bit of scenery at Cumberland, which he had hoped to see. This could not be helped, however, for by the train he would be set down in Cincinnati in good season for the important one-day session of a committee, the primary object of the trip.

To be sure, he would have to miss another important committee meeting at home, unless he should forego the Washington stop. But would it not be worth while to miss one of the meetings when he did not see how he could well arrange for both?

The ticket was bought and reservation was made. Then interruption number one came. Most unexpectedly there was a call from a neighbor to render such a service as can be given but once in a lifetime. Yet that difficult service must be rendered at the moment when, according to program, he would be taking the train for Washington.

Of course there could be no question as to his course. Instead of going to Washington and seeing the man with whom conference would mean so much, he must take train by a route more direct. This would enable him to reach Cincinnati in season for the committee meeting; and it would enable him also to attend the committee meeting at home which he had decided to put aside for the sake of the Washington opportunity.

After serving his neighbor and attending the home meeting—this turned out to be so important that to miss it would have been little short of a calamity—the direct train for Cincinnati was taken, though not without a sigh for the lost opportunity in Washington.

Yet the sigh was forgotten when on that train he became acquainted with three fellow-passengers who gave him some new and needed glimpses of life.

A study of time tables showed him that he could return by way of Washington, and could have two hours for the interview there on which he had counted so much, before the hour came for completing the homeward journey.

After a successful committee meeting in Cincinnati, the importance of which proved to be even greater than had been anticipated, the train for Washington was taken at the Cincinnati terminal. At the moment this train was due to leave, there drew in on an adjoining track cars from which weary, anxious-looking passengers alighted. "What train is that?" was the question that came to his lips.

"Number two, boss," the porter replied. "Left Washington at four yesterday afternoon. She's ten hours late, 'count of that big wreck down in the mountains."

And that was the train he had planned to take after finishing his business in Washington! If he had taken it, what of his touch with the Cincinnati meeting?

In thankful spirit, and with the resolve renewed for the ten thousandth time that he would cease to question God's wisdom in thwarting his little plans, he went to his berth. First, however, he included in his evening prayer a petition that the train might not be late in reaching Washington, since the time there would be short enough, at best.

Three hours later he roused with the start that is apt to come with the intense silence that marks a long night wait of a train between stations. The delay was so prolonged that soon the time table showed the loss of three hours.

There was one consolation, however: he would be able to pass during hours of daylight through the incomparable mountains of West Virginia.

The unexpected blessing was forgotten when the train drew into the Washington station so near the close of the afternoon that the traveler thought he might as well go home at once. Later on, he might be able to make a special trip to the Capital. "And I might have finished my program without all that expense and trouble," he thought.

But while he was there he decided he would call on the telephone the man in the department whom he wished to see. He told the man of his late train and his disappointment.

"Perhaps it is just as well," was the word from the other end of the wire. "I have been afraid that the time set aside for our work this afternoon was altogether too short. What do you say to coming to me the first thing in the morning? Then we can devote to our program all the time that proves necessary."

So he remained overnight. The evening gave him the chance he had sought for a year to spend an evening consulting authorities at the Congressional Library. Next morning the real business of the stopover was attended to. Then he learned why it would have been impossible to receive the afternoon before the attention he received during the morning hours. He knew, too, that it would have been out of the question to seek a second interview on the same business; therefore he would have had to rest content with the results of the first conference.

The time came to take the train for the final stage of the journey. On that train his seat-mate, a man he had never seen before, perhaps never would see again, gave him a number of bits of vital information on the very business that had led him to Washington!

Is it worth while to ask God to look out for the everyday needs of His people?

"BE strong and of a good courage!" More than three thousand years ago the inspiring words were spoken by a great military leader to men about to undertake a tremendous task. Some of them were dismayed. The difficulties in the path appeared insurmountable. Their minds were filled with worries and fears and anxieties, until the present was heavy with doubt and the future loomed before them dread, angry, portentous. Their hearts were like water, until Joshua, the leader, with great confidence gave his message:

> "Be strong and of a good courage—
> "Only be strong and very courageous—
> "Have not I commanded thee?
> "Be strong and of a good courage.
> "For Jehovah thy God is with thee
> whithersoever thou goest."

I
THAT'S FOR ME!

Two men were going around the marvelous horseshoe curve on the Tyrone and Clearfield Division of the Pennsylvania Railroad when one called the attention of his companion to the most picturesque part of the way.

"I was looking at that precipice when I had my first understanding of the fact that the Bible is a personal message; that I had the right to appropriate its words to my own life.

"It was the summer following the end of my final year in college. A few months earlier I had reluctantly yielded to the urging, first of my physician, then of a nerve specialist, by turning my back on college at the vital portion of the year. They told me that if I persisted in remaining they would not answer for the consequences; they said I had applied myself unwisely to my books until my brain was in revolt. 'It is a grave question if you will ever be able to take the professional course to which you have been looking forward,' the specialist said. 'One thing is certain, however: if you do not do as you are told you will not do any real brain work the rest of your days.'

"That scared me, for my heart was wrapped up in my plans for the future. I felt that life would not be worth while without some sort of active brain work. So I gave myself to a real bit of vacation. For months I cut myself loose from all books except the little copy of the Testament and Psalms which I carried with me more for form's sake than for any other reason, I fear. Daily as I tramped here and there in the wilds I read a verse or two, more because I thought I ought to do this than because I had any idea of receiving help.

"Toward the close of the summer I submitted myself to a specialist who shook his head, at the same time declaring that it was doubtful if even yet I could go on with my plan. He wouldn't say it was impossible for me to do brain work, but he urged that the probabilities were against me. A second specialist told me the same thing.

"So I faced the future as all summer long I had feared to face it. Finally my mind was made up to turn my back on professional studies. When the decision was made a suggestion came that I go into the mountains of Pennsylvania to investigate opportunity for a sort of work that I might do.

"The journey was begun. As we left Tyrone to climb the mountains my spirits sank lower and lower. I rebelled against the idea of taking the offered opening. How I longed to enter professional school in two weeks! But I dared not do it. To be sure, the physicians said that they saw no reason why I should not, though they feared the result. Why not try it? I had used all available means for restoration of the brain to the old-time keenness. Yet it would be awful to try and fail. No, I did not dare.

"So I was in the depths when my hand touched the pocket Testament and Psalms. Mechanically the book was opened, probably because of the unconscious realization that the daily portion had not yet been read. But listlessness was gone in an instant when my eyes fell on the words of Psalm 37:5:

"'Commit thy way unto the Lord; trust also in Him, and He will bring it to pass.'

"At first the words dazed me. Then I said: 'That's for me, and I'll do it! I've spent the summer as the doctors said I must. Surely I am warranted in committing myself unto the Lord in just the way the Psalm says. Of course I can't be sure that the result of going back to school will be precisely what I hope; but I can trust, and do my best. Then if the attempt results in failure, I shall have the satisfaction of knowing that I am following Him to whom I have committed my way.

"Some of my friends thought it was folly to begin my professional course. Can you imagine my joy when, from the day school opened, I had no recurrence of my trouble? Of course I was very careful until I could feel sure of my health."

"How do you explain your ability to go on with your studies?" his companion asked.

"I am not trying to explain it," was the reply. "But without question the assurance that came to me with that text from the Psalm, the assurance that God is my God and that I have a right to count on Him, made me strong to face things to which I had been unequal only a few months before.

"And is it strange that I have often wondered if there would have been any breakdown in college, if I had only known a little sooner of the strength that waits for those who, while putting forth their own utmost endeavor, at the same time count on God's unfailing strength?"

II
BANKING ON GOD'S PROMISES

Isn't it strange that so many Christians while believing, theoretically, in the reality and trustworthiness of God's promises, do not have the same sort of practical belief in Him which they show in the promise of their bank to pay them, on demand, the sum written down in their book of deposit?

And banks have been known to fail in keeping their very limited promises, while God has never failed in keeping His unlimited assurances of blessing.

For so many the strange delusion that God's promises are not to be counted on in the same literal sense as the promises of our associates persists through life, but there are fortunate Christians who have their eyes opened to the truth. And what a difference the knowledge makes to them!

F. B. Meyer told in one of his public addresses of the transformation wrought for him when his eyes were opened to the truth. As a boy of thirteen he had been a student at Brighton College. He was timid and sensitive, and the older students soon learned that they could make his life a burden to him. With a sigh of relief he went home at the end of the first week of school. On Sunday, however, the thought that he must return came to him with oppressing force. How could he stand up against the older students? He was idly turning the pages of his Bible when he came to the 121st Psalm. "How voraciously I devoured it!" he said. "How I read it again and again, and wrapt it round me! How I took it as my shield! And the next day I walked into the great expanse in front of the college so serene and strong. It was my first act of appropriating the promises of God."

Three years later the student was agonizing because he wanted to be a minister, yet feared to plan for the work because his voice was weak, and he feared that he would not have the courage to speak. He had been asking God to show him His will, and to help him in his difficulty. Then he found Jeremiah 1:7, and read it for the first time. "With indescribable feelings I read it again and again, and even now never come on it without a thrill of emotion," he said of his experience. "It was the answer to all my perplexing questionings. Yes, I was the child; I was to go to those to whom He sent me, and speak what He bade me, and He would be with me and teach my lips."

Another man, who had learned to accept literally God's promise, "Ask, and it shall be given unto you," wrote gratefully of his experience:

"My life is one long, daily, hourly record of answered prayer. For physical health, for mental overstrain, for guidance given marvelously, for errors and dangers averted, for enmity to the Gospel subdued, for food provided at the exact hour needed, for everything that goes to make up life and my poor service, I can testify with a full and often wonder-stricken awe that I believe God answers prayer. I know God answers prayer. Cavillings, logical or physical, are of no avail to me. It is the very atmosphere in which I live and breathe and have my being, and it makes life glad and free and a million times worth living."

A worker among his fellows in India stated the ground of his belief in God's promise to supply the needs of his people. The sentence was written while he was at home on furlough:

"Whatsoever you ask, believe that you have received it, and you shall have it. The belief is not the denial of a fact, but rather the assurance that the petition is in accordance with God's will, and that He is as disposed to give as we to receive; our reception of the gift depends on our holding on to His will. Now the practical question is, What is God's will? Am I conforming to it? Through lack of faith am I failing to receive and appropriate for myself and Satara what I and Satara need? Is it God's will that I should return and that there should be better paid work? More of it? More school-houses? New houses for workers?"

A few days later he added to these notes the word "Yes." His faith enabled him to claim God's promise.

A Christian young man in Japan was accustomed to stand at the entrance to the park in Tokyo, offering Bibles and preaching the Gospel. Years passed, and he saw no results of his work. Yet he believed in Him who had promised that His name should be exalted among the heathen. At length a Testament was bought by a young man to whom the words of John 3:16 brought life and joy. He went back to the old man from whose hand he had received the book, and told him that he had become a Christian. The man was overcome with joy.

"Ten years," he said, "I have been selling New Testaments here at the park gates, and you are the first who has ever come to tell me you were helped."

But throughout those ten years the faithful worker was sustained by his belief in the faithfulness of Him who had promised to bless him in his work. He knew that God would not fail him.

III
PRACTICAL PRECEPTS FROM PROVERBS

There is nothing like the Bible to put heart into a man. This is not strange, for the Book was written for this purpose by men of God's choosing whose business it was to strengthen their fellows.

One of the most vivid parts of the Bible is the book of Proverbs.

"Would that our young men were saturated with its thought," Albert J. Beveridge said of it, while he was a member of the United States Senate. "It is rich in practical wisdom for the minute affairs of practical life. It abounds in apt and pointed suggestions and pungent warnings concerning our companionship, our personal habits, our employments, our management of finance, our speech, the government of tongue and temper, and many other such things, which daily perplex the earnest soul, and daily occasion harm to the thoughtless and misguided."

Years earlier, another eminent American, Washington Irving, used what is the keynote of the book in an earnest talk with George Bancroft, later the historian of his country, then a student in Europe. The two were taking a walking excursion, when the older man said something the student remembered all his life. It was natural, then, that Bancroft's biographer should give this in his subject's own words, in "Life and Letters of George Bancroft:"

"At my time of life, he tells me, I ought to lay aside all care, and only be bent on laying in a stock of knowledge for future application. If I have not pecuniary resources enough to get at what I would wish for, as calculated to be useful to my mind, I must still not give up the pursuit. Still follow it; scramble to it; get at it as you can, but be sure to get at it. If you need books, buy them; if you are in want of instruction in anything take it. The time will soon come when it will be too late for all these things."

More than a century ago an immigrant from Scotland landed in New York. In the story of his life he later told how the book of Proverbs became his rock. The first night he slept in an old frame building with a shingle roof. During the night he was aroused by a storm of rain accompanied by thunder and lightning such as he had never experienced in Scotland. Homesick, terrified, unable to sleep, he rose and took from his chest the Bible his father had carefully packed with his clothes. He wrote later that as the book was opened, "My eyes fell on the words, 'My Son.' I was thinking of my father. I read on with delight. Having finished the last verse I found I had been reading the third chapter of the Proverbs of Solomon. Get a Bible and read the chapter. Then suppose yourself in my situation—sore in body, sick at heart, and commencing life among a world of strangers, and see if words more suitable could be put together to fit my case. I looked upon it as a chart from heaven, directing my course among the rocks, shoals and storms of life. . . . I went forth with a light heart to work my way through the world, resolved to keep this chapter as a pilot by my side."

The importance for to-day of the message in Proverbs 30:8, "Remove far from me vanity and lies," is illustrated by several incidents told by Lucy Elliot Keeler, in "If I Were a Boy:"

"The son of a distinguished American recently entered business in New York, beginning, at his father's request, at the foot of the ladder, and receiving the princely salary of $20 a month. At a time when his father's name was in everybody's mouth the editor of a yellow journal sent for the son and invited him to join the staff. 'You need not write any articles,' he said, with a smile, 'nor do any reporting. Just sign your name to an article which I will furnish you each day, and I will pay you $200 a month. . . .' The young man's reply was too emphatic to be accurately reported here, but it was to the effect that he would rather starve than pick untold dollars out of the gutter.

"A few years ago an American commissioner occupying a house in the West Indies hired a man to wash the windows and another to scrub the floors. The bills submitted were for $12 and $7, respectively. 'What does this mean?' was the astonished query. '$12 for a day's work? Man, you are crazy!' 'Oh,' came the soft reply, 'of course, I only expect a dollar and a half for myself, but that was the way we always made out bills for the Spanish officers.' 'Take back your bills,' was the American's emphatic reply, 'and make them out honestly.'"

The wisdom of the warning in Proverbs 27:2, "Let another man praise thee, and not thine own mouth," has seldom been more strikingly illustrated than at a large convention when several thousand people listened attentively as a speaker of reputation was introduced to them. He talked fluently for several minutes, then began to ramble. He made several attempts to regain his lost hold on his hearers, then took his seat.

"I can't imagine what was wrong to-day," he said to his neighbor on the platform. "I had all ready what I felt sure would be a telling address, but somehow I couldn't say what I wanted." A sympathetic answer was given by the man to whom he had spoken, but if he had said all that was in his heart this would have been his message: "I know you had a telling argument to present, for I read your manuscript. But you spent the first three minutes in talking about yourself. It was there you lost the attention of the people; they did not come to hear about you, but to learn of your Master. And when you had put yourself in the foreground, it was impossible for you to present Him with power."

The speaker's mistake is repeated every day, not merely by men on the platform, but by everyday people in the home, in the school, and at work. It is fatal to usefulness to put ourselves in the foreground; but those who forget self and remember others are welcome wherever they go.

IV
GETTING CLOSE TO THE BIBLE

One of the blessings that came to the world out of the anguish of the Great War was a new appreciation of God's Word on the part of many who had never paid much attention to the inspired Book, and the formation of the habit of Bible reading by tens of thousands of those who were once heedless of God's Word.

Absence from home in hours of danger, privation and suffering, opened the way for testing Him who reveals his power to give infinite blessing by saying tenderly, "As one whom his mother comforteth, so will I comfort you." The sense of absolute powerlessness in the face of barbarism led to dependence upon God who holds the worlds in His hands. Realization of the uncertainty of life and familiarity with death made easy and natural the approach to the Lord of life and death.

Probably there were soldiers who laughed at the words of Field Marshal Lord Roberts, spoken when the first British troops were crossing the Channel:

"You will find in this little Book (the Bible) guidance when you are in health, comfort when you are in sickness, and strength when you are in adversity," but the day came when one of the soldiers themselves, Arthur Guy Empey, wrote:

"How about the poor boy lying wounded, perhaps dying, in a shell hole, his mother far away? Perhaps to him even God seems to have forgotten; he feels for his first-aid packet, binds up his wounds, and then waits—years, it seems to him—for the stretcher-bearers. Then he gets out his Testament; the feel of it gives him comfort and hope. He reads. That boy gets religion, even though when he enlisted he was an atheist."

A Young Men's Christian Association secretary told of an incident when the soldiers were just leaving for the trenches. "He saw a young lad nervously making his way up to the counter. He knew the boy wanted something, and was afraid to ask or was timid about it. He said, 'Want something, lad?' 'Yes, sir, I have got a Bible and I don't know much about it. I'd like you to mark some passages in it. I am going out to the trenches to-night.' 'Sure!' said the secretary. 'Mark some good ones, now,' said the lad.

"While he was marking the first lad's book half a dozen other boys came up and said, 'Mark mine, too, sir!' And for half an hour this secretary was busy marking verses in the Bibles of those boys. An interested observer asked him what he marked, and he said, 'Matthew 10:23; 11:28; 6:19, 20; John 3:16; Romans 8:35-39.'"

"Fighting" Pat O'Brian, of the Royal Fighting Corps, whose marvelous escape from his German captors thrilled multitudes, said:

"I haven't been given to talking much about religion, but when, after two months of flight through an enemy country as an escaped prisoner, going without food except such as I could pick up in the fields and eat raw, and time and again coming within a hair's breadth of being caught, I finally got through the lines on to the neutral soil of Holland, I was mighty glad to get down on my knees and thank God that He had got me through. A lot of men who have never thought much about religion are thinking about it now. I believe they will read those little khaki Testaments, and I am sure they will get help from them."

That "those little khaki Testaments" were going into the hands of the soldiers pleased General Pershing, who said, "Its teachings will fortify us for our great task." And Secretary of the Navy Daniels rejoiced that the books were going to the sailors, for he said, "The Bible is the one book from which men can find help and inspiration and encouragement for whatever conditions may arise."

V
THE BIBLE AND ONE MAN

In June, 1862, John E. Clough was graduated from an Iowa college. He had been eager to make a name for himself. Many promising avenues of secular work had opened to him, and he had tried to take one or another of them. But always he knew that it was not right for him to plan for anything but the ministry. The impression was deepened when the president of the college took for the text of his baccalaureate sermon, "For none of us liveth to himself, and no man dieth to himself." So the young graduate left the college feeling that he was no longer free to go out and use his education for the career he had dreamed of.

But he did decide to teach for a year. With Mrs. Clough, he made an engagement to teach a public school one year. But he did not dare stay for a second year, because the people were so good to the new teacher, and there was so much evidence of this popularity, that the Bible words kept ringing in his ears, "Woe unto you when all men shall speak well of you." He knew he was not in the right place. In later life, when opposition came to him because he was doing faithful Christian work, he was strengthened by the memory of this text that had once been anything but a comfort to him.

At last came the beginning of the work in India that made the name of John E. Clough famous. His success was due, in large measure, to the fact that he emphasized God's Word. One of his first acts was to prepare a tract in Scripture language, telling the things necessary for salvation, and this proved useful throughout his services.

Everywhere he went he quoted Scripture to the people. He felt that whatever else he might say to them, this would be most effective. One text was used more than any other, in private conversation and in sermons, the invitation of Jesus, "Come unto me, all ye that labor and are heavy laden, and I will give you rest." This, he said, was always new, and the people received his explanations gladly. Once, during a time of grievous famine, when about them millions of the natives died of want and disease, these words proved especially effective.

As a measure of famine relief the missionary took the contract for a section of the great Buckingham Canal. Under his leadership the natives were set to work on this. Native evangelists as well as white missionaries toiled day after day, and this gave a splendid chance for preaching the gospel. "The name of Jesus was spoken all day long from one end of our line to the other," Mr. Clough wrote in his autobiography. "The preachers carried a New Testament in their pockets. It comforted the people to see the holy book of the Christians amid all their distress. They said, when they sat down for a short rest, 'Read us again out of your holy book about the weary and heavy laden.' That verse, 'Come unto me all ye that labor,' was often all I had to give the people by way of comfort. The preachers were saying it all day long. It carried us through the famine. We all needed it, for even the strongest among us sometimes felt our courage sinking."

All through Dr. Clough's missionary career there was one verse in particular that carried him far. When he was out on tour among the people, often many miles distant from home, Mrs. Clough was accustomed to send after him a messenger who would take to him, for his encouragement, the message she felt he needed. Knowing his fondness for the text, "Be still, and know that I am God; I will be exalted among the heathen," she sent the words to him on more than one occasion. In the story of his life he told of a day when the text came to him with special force:

"I was tempted to shake the dust off my feet and go. My helpers and I had camped in a new place, and had been trying hard to get the people to come and listen to the gospel, but they would not. I concluded that it was a hard place, and told my staff of workers that we were justified in leaving it alone and moving on elsewhere. Toward noon I went into my tent, closed down the sides, let the little tent flap swing over my head, and rested, preparatory to starting off for the next place. Just then a basket of supplies was brought to my feet by a coolie, who had walked seventy miles with the basket on his head. In the accompanying letter Mrs. Clough quoted my favorite verse to me. While reading this, some of the preachers put their heads into the tent and said, 'Sir, there is a big crowd out here; the grove is full; all are waiting for you. Please come out.'"

Once the two verses that were the keynote of the missionary's life were especially prominent. For a long time he had been discouraged because results seemed slow and difficulties were great. But the day came when he stood before thousands and preached to them the Word, strong in the assurance of the presence of Him who said, "Be still, and know that I am God: I will be exalted among the heathen." The text that day, as so often before, was "Come unto me, all ye that labor and are heavy laden." For an hour the people listened to his words. Then they began to plead for baptism, and would not be denied. At length, after rigid examination, baptism was administered to 3,536 within three days. And he had not baptized one soul in fifteen months before this time!

God's Word gave courage to Clough; it enabled him to give courage to others; and it will give courage to you.

VI
OUT OF THE DEPTHS

During the year 1538 an Italian spent long weeks in a noisome underground prison cell, where he was kept on account of religious differences. For a precious hour and a half of each day, when the light struggled in through a tiny window, he read the Bible, especially the Psalms. Among the Psalms that meant most to him was the one hundred and thirtieth, whose beginning "Out of the depths have I cried unto thee, O Lord," expressed the longings of his heart for companionship and comfort.

Exactly two hundred years later, on May 24, 1738, John Wesley, then in the midst of the greatest anxiety and longing for God, heard the choir at St. Paul's Cathedral sing, "Out of the depths have I cried unto thee, O Lord." The words brought joy to him. From the depths in which he found himself that afternoon he cried unto God, and that evening there came to him the knowledge of God's presence that gave him strength to begin the wonderful work that built up the great Methodist Church.

These same words meant much to Josiah Royce, the American teacher of philosophy, who died in 1916. In one of his later books, he wrote:

"We come to such deep places that we can only cry. We are astonished that we can cry. And then we become aware that our cry is heard. And he who hears is God. And so God is often defined for the plain man as 'He who hears man's cry from the depths.'"

One who knew Professor Royce well wondered if he did not enter the depths from which he cried to God and received such satisfying response, after the death of his only son. In the same way those who delight in the message of Psalm 130 wonder what could have been the experience of depression that opened the way for his reception of God's blessing.

We can only speculate about these things. But there is one thing of which we can be absolutely sure: there is no depth so low that the cry of one of God's children will not reach from it to the heart of the Father; no sorrow so crushing, no anxiety so overwhelming, no pain so intense, no difficulty seemingly so unsolvable, no sin so awful, that eager, earnest prayer will not bring God to the relief of the sufferer.

"If out of the depths we cry, we shall cry ourselves out of the depths," one has said who has written of the words that Professor Royce found so helpful. Then he asks: "What can a man do who finds himself at the foot of a beetling cliff, the sea in front, the wall of rock at his back, without foothold for a mouse, between the tide at the bottom and the grass at the top? He can do but one thing, he can shout, and, perhaps, may be heard, and a rope may come dangling down that he can spring at and catch. For sinful men in the miry pit the rope is already let down, and their grasping it is the same as the psalmist's cry. God has let down His forgiving love in Christ, and we need but the faith which accepts it while it asks, and then we are swung up into the light, and our feet set on a rock."

Each one has depths peculiarly his own, and longs to be out of them. Then why not call to Him who hears men's cry from the depths, with the quiet confidence of quaint old Herbert, who wrote:

> Of what an easie quick accesse,
>   My blessed Lord, art Thou! how suddenly

May our requests thine ears invade!
If I but lift mine eyes my suit is made;
Thou canst no more not heare than Thou
canst die.

Printed in the USA
CPSIA information can be obtained
at www.ICGtesting.com
LVHW080146110524
779587LV00010B/354